JN102664

Hope: Beyond Kyushu

日本から世界へ 発信するコミュニケーション

Yoshihiro Kubo
Tim Cross

EIHŌSHA

はじめに

　英語で円滑にコミュニケーションを行うためには，英語という言語自体の知識とその知識を実際の場面で使う技能の両方が必要です．AI（Artificial Intelligence）技術の発達により，前者の知識は補えるでしょうが，後者の技能に関しては，コミュニケーションは人間同士が行うわけですから，コミュニケーションが円滑に行われるためにはAI技術が補えない部分があります．従って，英語という言語を使って円滑にコミュニケーションを行うには，英語そのものの知識はもちろんのこと，その知識を実際の場面で使う技能も大切になってきます．

　そこで，本書は前者の知識の増強のため，各ユニットの前半は，九州各県と日本の言語文化に関するトリビア（学生が感心する内容）をテーマにしたパッセージを中心に，そのパッセージの読解に必要な語彙と文法の知識を土台に，読解力を養成します．一方，後者の技能の向上のため，各ユニットの後半は，実際の場面で使えるライティング，スピーキングの技能の養成を目指しています．リーディング，リスニング，ライティング，スピーキングの4技能の総合的な養成とバラエティーに富むエクササイズを通して，九州から，そして日本から世界に向け，発信できるようなコミュニケーション能力を養成していこうというのが本書のねらいです．

　読む，聞く，話す，書く，の作業を通じて，語彙と文法の力の増強ばかりではなく日常的な英語表現の習得や異文化に対するさらなる理解にもつながるように，自らあるいはグループで調べてプレゼンをするといった多種多様なエクササイズを設けて，英語という言語の知識を実際の場面で運用できる力を養成していきます．その目標達成に向けての本書の構成は以下の通りです．

Vocabulary Quiz：パッセージの内容理解に必要な語彙力のチェックを行い，語彙力の増強を図ります．

Grammar Check：パッセージの内容理解につながるような文法事項のチェックを行い，文法力の増強を図ります．

Passage：パッセージは，九州各県を中心としたトリビアと日本の大学生が感心する内容をテーマにしています．パッセージのテーマに関しては，以下のCross氏によるPrefaceをご一読ください．学習者はパッセージを読む際はパラグラフ毎の要点を理解するように努めてください．そのことによって，内容把握を主眼とした英語読解力の養成につながります．このような内容把握型の読解力は，TOEIC，TOEFLのリーディングセクションの問題を解く際にも重要です．

Comprehension Questions：パッセージのパラグラフ毎の要点を理解するために，パラグラフ毎に内容把握問題を課し，パッセージ全体の内容の理解につなげます．

Dialogue：ディクテーションのエクササイズを通して口語表現を学習します．

TOEIC Challenge：TOEICのListening Sectionの問題に慣れるため同形式の問題を設定し，TOEIC対策を講じています．DialogueとTOEIC Challengeによってリスニング力の強化を図ります．

Useful Expressions for Conversation：Dialogueで用いられた表現，あるいは関連した口語

表現の習得を目指します．口語表現は，いずれもコミュニカティブ・ファンクションを中心として，実際の場面ですぐ用いられるものばかりです．

Practical Use：Useful Expressions for Conversation で学習した表現を実際の場面で使えるように，日常会話表現を英語で書く練習をします．その後，学習者はペアになって，英語で会話の練習をするようにしてください．この書く，話す，の訓練を通じて，発信能力の養成を図ります．

Little Quiz：パッセージの内容に関連する英語を効率よく運用する上での豆知識の学習のために，個人あるいはグループで調べてプレゼンをするという形式にしています．

本書の多種多様な形式の問題を通して，楽しく且つ活気のある授業が展開され，その結果として，本書を使って学習するみなさんの英語の知識とそれを運用する力の両方が向上することを願っています．

久保　善宏

Don't think of this book as just an English textbook ...

What is hope? Do you think that hope is an emotion that only some people can feel? Instead of thinking that hope is an emotion that a few lucky people feel every day, researchers have found that it is better to think about the process of creating hope. Once we have learned how to control that process, mastering the process of creating hope means Japanese students can get better academic grades, develop stronger friendships between themselves and with international exchange students, and show more creativity and better problem-solving skills when faced with obstacles to their progress.

The student activists from Hokkaido all the way down to Okinawa who appear in this book are hopeful students. Although they are trying to improve Japan in many different ways (the environment, health and diet, blood donations, etc), these students don't take failure personally. They use the experience of not being successful to improve what they do the next time. When they are facing some trouble, being hopeful means that they can say to themselves, "I can do this. I can find a way to move forward because I won't give up."

How can you tell if those researchers would think that you are a hopeful student?

    1 Do you set clear goals and deadlines that you can realistically achieve?

    2 Do you use more than one strategy to reach your goals by their deadline?

Hopeful students know how to do these two things, and keep using their strategies to achieve their goals, even when they are having trouble moving forwards.

The science of hope is more than just wishfully thinking "I wish I could win the lottery and spend the money by going kitesurfing in Sri Lanka with all my classmates tomorrow, instead of having to take that English test!" Hope is a way of thinking where we set goals and deadlines as we work toward them by checking our progress, one small step at a time.

If we want to build these skills of hope, here are three points for you.

1) What are your top goals, from big to small?

Start by making a list of what's important to you—such as hobbies, friends, family, sport, or career—and then think about which of those important areas can make you feel the most satisfied. Next, using this list, try to create specific goals that are a positive, solutions-oriented approach. Don't start with something negative ("I will stop texting when I drink-drive!"). Instead, please choose a future achievement: "I will make more friends by taking a class to learn another second language." Finally, ranking your goals in order of importance will help you focus your time and energy on the goals that can have the greatest impact on your happiness.

2) Can you break those goals—especially long-term ones—into smaller steps?

If you can see your bigger goals as a series of smaller steps, you will feel the joy of progress as you celebrate your steps of gradual success.

3) What are some of the different ways to reach your goal?

We all meet some trouble as we try to achieve our goals. Being flexible enough to try a different path to success often begins with imagining the barriers you need to overcome.

Being hopeful just means that you believe you can get what you want and you will keep trying to move to your goals, especially when you are facing those challenges called obstacles.

Tim Cross

テキストの音声は、弊社 HP　https://www.eihosha.co.jp/
の「テキスト音声ダウンロード」のバナーからダウンロードできます。
また、下記 QR コードを読み込み、音声ファイルをダウンロードするか、
ストリーミングページにジャンプして音声を聴くことができます。

Contents

.

Unit 1

Kyushu Rocks: Putting Kyushu on the Map

Vocabulary Quiz ［**Passage** 読解のための語彙力チェック］

空所に入れるのに適した単語を, a ~ d の中から選び丸をつけましょう.

1. divide the students _____ groups of five （学生を 5 人ずつに分ける）
   a. in　　　b. into　　　c. to　　　d. on

2. Nagasaki is _____ Kyushu. （長崎は九州にある）
   a. at　　　b. on　　　c. to　　　d. into

3. the _____ of Quebec （ケベック州）
   a. Province　b. Prefecture　c. State　d. Nation

4. Fukuoka _____ （福岡県）
   a. Province　b. Prefecture　c. State　d. Nation

5. a suitcase _____ wheels （車輪付きのスーツケース）
   a. at　　　b. in　　　c. on　　　d. off

6. a five-_____ truck （5 トントラック）
   a. ton　　　b. tons　　　c. ton of　　　d. tons of

Grammar Check ［**Passage** 読解のための文法力チェック］

1. 「博多祇園山笠では,」という和文を英訳すると, 次のいずれが適切ですか？

   Teams of men carry a one ton float five kilometers in the Hakata Gion Yamakasa of Fukuoka.

   In the Hakata Gion Yamakasa of Fukuoka, teams of men carry a one ton float five kilometers.

2. 次の文で to be が省略できるのはいずれですか？

   He seems to be kind.

   He seems to be a college student.

3. 自分の答えの方が正しいと思っている時, 「君の答えが正しいなら, 僕の答えは間違っていることになる.」を英訳すると, 次のいずれが適切ですか？

   If your answer is right, my answer is wrong. （for a question with only two correct choices）

   If your answer was right, my answer would be wrong.

Passage Kyushu

When you ask foreigners the best place to visit in Japan, you never hear 'Kyushu'. For many foreign tourists, Tokyo, Osaka and Kyoto are Japan. Some foreigners know where Kyushu is after you say 'Nagasaki is on Kyushu'.

外国人にとって九州とは？

Most foreigners don't realize that Kyushu is more exciting than Tokyo, Osaka and Kyoto. Kyoto has its Gion Yamakasa, but in that festival, everything moves smoothly on wheels. In the Hakata Gion Yamakasa of Fukuoka, teams of men carry a one ton float five kilometers. Watching the summertime power of Hakata men seems a lot more interesting to many foreigner visitors than the slow rhythm of Kyoto.

京都祇園山笠 vs. 博多祇園山笠

Hardly any foreign visitors know that Kyushu means 'nine provinces'. If you meet a foreign tourist who can tell you the names of those original provinces (Saikaidou was divided into Chikuzen, Chikugo, Bizen, Higo, Buzen, Bungo, Hyuga, Osumi, Satsuma), it is always interesting to ask them to explain how those nine provinces became seven prefectures (Fukuoka, Kagoshima, Kumamoto, Miyazaki, Nagasaki, Oita, Saga) in 1972.

九州って州が九つあるの？

注：**float** 山車（だし）　**province** 州：日本で古くから用いられた地域区分の一つで，一行政区画の国（例：奥州，信州）

Comprehension Questions

Based on the Passage, please choose the best answer.

1. What does the first paragraph say about foreign tourists?

    A. All foreign tourists love the tradition of Kyoto.

    B. Some foreign tourists recommend Kyushu as the best place to visit in Japan.

    C. Many foreign visitors have a narrow understanding of Japan.

    D. Most foreign visitors know where to find Nagasaki on a map of Japan.

2. What does the second paragraph say about Fukuoka?

    A. All foreign tourists think the tradition of Kyoto is better than anything in Fukuoka.

    B. Hakata Yamakasa is more dynamic than the quieter Kyoto Gion.

    C. The Hakata Gion Yamakasa of Fukuoka goes smoothly because of the wheels of the float.

    D. The festivals of Tokyo, Osaka and Kyoto are no more exciting than what happens in Fukuoka.

3. What does the third paragraph say about foreign tourists?

    A. The details of Japanese history are a mystery to most foreign visitors.

    B. Many foreign visitors know that Kyushu means 'nine provinces'.

    C. Some foreign tourists think travel is important because it gives an education which is different from studying history books.

    D. A few foreign tourists can explain Kyushu means 'seven prefectures'.

Dialogue

次の対話を聞いて，下線部を埋めてみよう．

Mary: Foreign tourists are really changing Japan!

Bill: Really?

Mary: So many shops in Fukuoka have Chinese-speaking sales staff ₁_____ those huge luxury liners come to Hakata port with 4,000 Chinese people every week.

Bill: ₂_____! We do hear so much Chinese being spoken on the streets these days, ₃_____? But I wonder how long all this will last?

Mary: ₄_____ the yen is weak, I guess.

Bill: So Fukuoka schools better ₅_____ not being able to use buses for their schools trips because all local bus companies must work together when those Chinese ships arrive.

TOEIC Challenge

Based on the Dialogue, choose the best answer.

1. What are they talking about?

    A. Chinese language

    B. Chinese travelers

    C. Hints to travelers

    D. Hakata port

2. How did the man feel about the woman's opinion?

    A. He couldn't agree with her more.

    B. His opinion is different from hers.

    C. He can't agree with her one hundred percent.

D.　They don't see eye to eye.

Useful Expressions for Conversation

1.　確認・同意を求める：話し手が聞き手に自分の言った内容についての確認や同意を求める時に用いられる表現

次の文において，イタリック体の表現のイントネーションを上昇調にする時と下降調にする時の意味の違いは何ですか？

You don't like him, {*do you / right*}?

2.　同意する：相手の意見に同意を示す時に用いられる表現

次の文の中で，相手の意見に同意を示す時に用いられる表現はどれですか？
　　a.　You're right.
　　b.　There you go!
　　c.　I couldn't agree more.
　　d.　That's how I feel.
　　e.　That's the way to go.

Practical Use

以下の下線部に日本文の意味に合うように適切な語（句）を入れ，その後，ペアで読んでみましょう．
　　1.　「あなた，きのう飲みすぎたんじゃない？」
　　　　"You had one drink too many yesterday, _____?"

　　　　「その通り！」
　　　　"_____!"

　　2.　「このお店，インスタ映えするよね.」
　　　　"This shop would _____ great on Instagram."

　　　　「私もまさにそう思います.」
　　　　"That's _____ I feel."

Little Quiz

様々な数字の読み方

1. 次の数字，小数点，比率を英語で言ってみましょう．

    2,000,000

    3,000,000,000

    4,000,000,000,000

    3.14

    0.507

    1：3（1 対 3）

2. 次の電話番号と番地を英語で言ってみましょう．

    090-123-4567

    8-19-1 Nanakuma, Jonan-ku（城南区七隈 8 -19-1）

Unit 2 Surfing paradise!

Vocabulary Quiz

空所に入れるのに適した単語を，a～d の中から選び丸をつけましょう．

1. ＿＿＿＿＿＿＿ pumpkin cakes （美味しいパンプキンケーキ）
   a. yummy   b. mammy   c. pappy   d. sunny

2. a recipe ＿＿＿＿＿＿＿ tomato soup （トマトスープの調理法）
   a. of   b. for   c. on   d. with

3. Those bananas aren't ＿＿＿＿＿＿＿ yet. （あのバナナはまだ熟れていない）
   a. ripen   b. to ripen   c. ripe   d. ripely

4. feeling the sand ＿＿＿＿＿＿＿ my toes （僕の足の指の間にはさまる砂粒の感触）
   a. on   b. between   c. at   d. into

5. There was ＿＿＿＿＿＿＿ snow yesterday. （昨日記録的な降雪があった）
   a. record   b. recorded   c. recording d. recorder

6. ＿＿＿＿＿＿＿ a connection （関係づける，結びつけて考える）
   a. do   b. have   c. make   d. take

Grammar Check

1. 次の文の下線部にはそれぞれ looked at，watched のいずれが入りますか？

   We sat and ＿＿＿＿ the sunset. （日没を眺めた）
   We sat and ＿＿＿＿ the painting. （絵を眺めた）

2. -o で終わる名詞を複数形にする時，-s か -es にする決め手は何だと思いますか？

   heroes, potatoes, tomatoes, echoes, vetoes
   bamboos, radios, studios, cuckoos

   その決め手は次の語に当てはまりますか？
   autos, kilos, photos, pianos, memos

Passage Miyazaki

When I get that Miyazaki sand between my toes every summer, I always remember the UK punk band the Stranglers and their 1977 song about 'walking on the beaches, looking at the peaches.' That is a strange connection to make because Miyazaki is famous for mangoes, Chicken Nanban, and yummy pork Niku-Maki Onigiri, but not peaches.

宮崎の名産と言えば？

What is the recipe for success of the world-famous Miyazaki mangoes? As each mango ripens, its sugar level rises. All of the Sun Egg ('Taiyo no Tamago') mangoes that sell for record prices must have a sugar content of at least fifteen percent. Each one of those beautiful fruit is caught in a net as it drops off the tree. Those nets stop the mangoes from hitting the ground, and that is why the best-tasting fruit always look so perfect.

太陽のタマゴって知ってる？

The farmers wait for each mango to be perfectly ripe because that is when it naturally drops off the tree. Eating pork rice-balls for lunch before going home to a dinner of Chicken Nanban gave those Miyazaki farmers something more than the power to work hard every day. These men and women were tough: they worked for eight years without earning any money as they tried to grow the perfect mango of their dreams. Without their hard work from 1986, relaxing on the beach at Aoshima, enjoying that sweet taste after catching a few waves in the salty Pacific Ocean, would not be the same.

太陽のタマゴが熟すと？

注：**the Stranglers**　1975 年から活動を始めたイギリスのニューウェーブのロック
グループ　　**Aoshima**　青島：宮崎県南部の小島で，干潮時には陸続きになり，
「鬼の洗濯岩」と呼ばれる海食台地が現れる

Comprehension Questions

Based on the Passage, please choose the best answer.

1. What does the first paragraph say about Miyazaki?

    A. Miyazaki is a popular tourist stop for the punk bands of Great Britain.

    B. Delicious Miyazaki peaches are grown on those warm beaches.

    C. The power of music to travel across time and space can be felt on Miyazaki beaches.

    D. Miyazaki summer food mixes chicken, pork and fruit in one delicious dish.

2. What does the second paragraph say about what makes a perfect mango?
    A. The best mangoes must be harvested before the sun rises.
    B. When each mango is cut, the scissors must be held at fifteen degrees.
    C. Miyazaki fishermen use nets to harvest the mangoes as they shake the trees.
    D. The best mangoes must have a high sugar content and perfect skin.

3. What does the third paragraph imply about the best way for us to relax on Aoshima Beach after surfing?
    A. Forget work-life balance: without working hard, relaxation has no meaning.
    B. Eating a delicious mango there is the best way to relax after you get out of the ocean.
    C. The best way to relax on Aoshima Beach after surfing is to get back in the water and keep surfing, until you drop ...
    D. It is tough to relax on the beach after surfing because you are dreaming of eating pork rice-balls for dinner.

Dialogue

次の対話を聞いて，下線部を埋めてみよう．

Mary: Hey, great news! I ₁_____ study: one year of farm training, ₂_____ the Japan Agricultural Exchange Council. Somewhere in South America!

Bill: You're going to South America for a year?

Mary: No details from JAEC yet, but yes!

Bill: What are you trying to say? I'm sorry, but what does that ₃_____ for us?

Mary: ₄_____ am I trying to say? ₅_____, do you have a passport and can you speak Spanish?

Bill: Si, el pasaporte, OK!

TOEIC Challenge

Based on the Dialogue, choose the best answer.
    1. How long will Mary study abroad?
        A. One month
        B. Next year
        C. Half a year
        D. Twelve months

2. If Bill does exactly what Mary wants him to do, what will he do?
   A. He will make all the necessary arrangements for going abroad with her.
   B. He will get ready for going to Spain.
   C. He will study up for a Spanish exam.
   D. He will see the woman off.

Useful Expressions for Conversation

1. 理解していないことを示す：相手の言ったことを理解していないことを示す表現

   相手が，目上の人，初対面の人やあまり親しくない人の場合に，相手が言った後に，
   次のような表現を用いた場合，相手への印象はどうなるでしょうか？

   "What?" / "What did you say?"

2. 説明を求める：相手の言ったことを理解していない場合，自分が理解していないことを示
   した後の，相手に説明を求める表現.

   上記のような状況の場合，次のいずれの表現を用いますか？

   a. Could you say that again?
   b. Could you repeat it?
   c. Will you explain that?
   d. Where exactly are we to meet?
   e. What time did you say?

Practical Use

以下の下線部に日本文の意味に合うように適切な語（句）を入れ，その後，ペアで読んでみましょ
う.

1. 「今年の夏はマチュピチュに行くつもりです.」
   "This summer I'm _____ Machu Picchu."

   「えー，どこへ行くって？」
   "Oh, you're _____?"

2. 「私は新しい上司とうまが合わないみたい.」

"I don't seem to get _____ my new boss."

「それは具体的にはどういう意味ですか？」

"_____ do you mean?"

Little Quiz

These days we can order various regional specialties on the internet. Can you tell us about the *meisan* (specialty or special product) of your hometown? For example, "Sweet potatoes are a specialty of Kagoshima," "Peaches are a special product of Okayama," "The best-known specialty of Hiroshima is oysters," "The *amanatsu* oranges of Nokonoshima are to die for!", etc. Now give a quick presentation to other students on the specialty of your hometown using simple sentences.

Vocabulary Quiz

空所に入れるのに適した単語を，a 〜 d の中から選び丸をつけましょう．

1. the ＿＿＿＿＿＿＿＿＿＿ （僧侶，聖職者）
   a. priest　　　b. priestly　　　c. ministry　　　d. ministership

2. ＿＿＿＿＿＿＿＿＿＿ prayers （祈りの言葉を詠唱する）
   a. sing　　　b. chorus　　　c. chant　　　d. pray

3. ＿＿＿＿＿＿＿＿＿＿ water （水をはねかける）
   a. spray　　　b. splash　　　c. jet　　　d. fire

4. ＿＿＿＿＿＿＿＿＿＿ traditional and current ideas （伝統的な考えと現代的な考えを一体にする）
   a. uniform　　　b. unify　　　c. union　　　d. unity

5. ＿＿＿＿＿＿＿＿＿＿ the idea objectively （その考えを客観的に解釈する）
   a. interpreter　　b. interpretable　　c. interpretation　　d. interpret

6. ＿＿＿＿＿＿＿＿＿＿ to that man （その人に対する不誠実）
   a. insincere　　b. sincere　　c. insincerity　　d. sincerity

Grammar Check

1. 数量詞 all が名詞 the men を修飾する場合，次のいずれが適切ですか？

   The men all chanted "oissa, oissa."

   They threw *kioimizu* water on the men all.

2. 次の文の主語は what と that のいずれで始めるのが適切ですか？

   { What / That } we now call the Hakata Gion Yamakasa had its beginning in 1241.

3. 特定の日や週を表す場合，それぞれ in と on のいずれが適切ですか？

   { In / On } the first day of school, I overslept.

   { In / On } the first week of July, disaster struck.

Let me try to surprise you: Japanese traditions survive because they change. What is now called the Hakata Gion Yamakasa had its beginning in 1241 when the plague was killing everyone. As the head priest of Jōten-ji was carried around Hakata on a *segaki-dana*, he chanted prayers and splashed holy water through the streets of Hakata. Now international tourists throw *kioimizu* water on the men carrying the shrines, who are powered by the rhythm of *kakegoe*.

Kakegoe are a central part of the spiritual soundscape of Japan that has kept hope alive for many generations. The power of the human voice unifies the hearts and minds of Hakata people. On the first day of July, when the *tōban chō* districts run to Hakozaki Shrine for *oshioi-tori*, gathering the beach sand that will protect them from injury, the men all chant "osshoi, osshoi." When this chant changes to "oissa, oissa" from the tenth day of July, when the *kakiyama* shrines are carried through Hakata, that tells us that the men are ready for the emotional intensities of the summer challenge of carrying their Yamakasa shrines five kilometers.

Kakegoe are one part of the Yamakasa tradition that was changed to allow this prayer-in-action *matsuri* to survive. Before COVID, if your *kakegoe* was not loud, that was interpreted as a sign of spiritual insincerity or weakness. After COVID, even the head priest of Kushida Shrine agreed that the men who have the *dai-agari* honour of sitting on the Yamakasa shrines and the responsibility of leading the *kakegoe* chorus of the men carrying the shrines should not use the full power of their voice. Along with shortening the length of the course over which the shrines would be carried, and reducing the number of men running in the *matsuri*, a quieter *kakegoe* was a small price to pay for restarting the Yamakasa tradition after two years of COVID silence. Traditions, like hope itself, must face the real world if they are to continue to inspire future generations.

伝統は生き残る？

祭りの掛け声は変化する？

博多祇園山笠の伝統は？

注：**Hakata Gion Yamakasa**：博多祇園山笠　　**Jōten-ji**：承天寺（福岡市博多区）
segaki-dana：施餓鬼棚　　**kioimizu**：勢水（きおいみず）　　**tōban chō**：当
番町　　**oshioi-tori**：お汐井取り（清めの真砂を竹製の枡やてぼにすくい取る）
kakiyama：舁き山　　**Kushida Shrine**：櫛田神社（博多総鎮守）
dai-agari：台あがり（山笠の前後にある台の上にすわり，舁き山の全体式を取る）

Based on the Passage, please choose the best answer.

1. What does the first paragraph say about traditions?
   A. Anything that is called a Japanese tradition must be at least 600 years old.
   B. Since the Meiji period, Japanese traditions have avoided foreign influences.
   C. If Japanese traditions are to continue, they must not stay exactly the same forever.
   D. Japanese traditions cure the sickness of modern Japan.

2. What does the second paragraph say about the traditional power of *kakegoe*?
   A. The spiritual soundscape of modern Japan is a postwar invention.
   B. The spiritual soundscape of Japan includes the *kakegoe* of parents protecting their children at the beach.
   C. *Kakegoe* were invented to help international tourists understand Japanese traditions.
   D. Even if *kakegoe* change during a *matsuri*, that unifying power stays the same.

3. What does the third paragraph say about traditions?
   A. Traditions must do whatever is necessary now to be part of future Japanese life.
   B. The spiritual weakness of the past shapes the future of Japanese traditions.
   C. The most honourable thing a tradition can do is stay the same forever.
   D. Shorter *matsuri* traditions are responsible for a better Japanese work-life balance.

Dialogue

次の対話を聞いて，下線部を埋めてみよう．

Jade: Please explain to the court why you were driving so fast in a school zone where the speed limit is 40 km/h.

Leo: I didn't want to be going at that speed but that driver ₁_____ was getting closer and closer. Just wouldn't stop! Creeping up behind me, getting so noisy, and so I was trying to just get away ... Your Honour, being over the speed limit wasn't my fault. My face was ₂_____, you see.

Jade: What kind of vehicle was behind you?

Leo: One of those Fukuoka City ₃_____. ₄_____ at normal people and ₅_____ their lights as we are just going about our normal daily business!

Based on the Dialogue, choose the best answer.

1. Who is Jade?

    A. Leo's friend

    B. A rescue squad leader

    C. A police officer

    D. A lawyer

2. How did Leo feel about the ambulance coming closer?

    A. He was frightened by being tailgated.

    B. He realized that the car behind him was creepy.

    C. He was happy to ride in that ambulance.

    D. He was so angry he wanted to tailgate the ambulance.

Useful Expressions for Conversation

1. 提示：相手の探し物や望みのものを渡す表現

    次の文の中で，相手の探し物や望みのものを「はい，どうぞ」と渡す時の表現として不適格なのはどれですか？

    a. Please.

    b. Here it is.

    c. Here you are.

    d. Here you go.

2. 非難：話し手の主観として非難や批判の気持ちが込められる表現

    次の文の中で，話し手の非難の気持ちが込められているのはどれですか？

    a. She chatted with her friends over coffee.

    b. She is chatting with her friends over coffee.

    c. She always chats with her friends over coffee.

    d. She is always chatting with her friends over coffee.

Practical Use

以下の下線部に日本文の意味に合うように適切な語（句）を入れ, その後, ペアで読んでみましょう.

1. 「ねえ, 一郎, そこのホチキス取ってくれる？」

   "Hey, Ichiro, can you pass me that _____?"

   「もちろん. はい, どうぞ.」
   "Sure. _____ ."

2. 「彼女は僕のためにせっせと家具付きのアパートを探してくれているんだ.」
   "She is going about looking for a furnished apartment for me."

   「あなたはいつも彼女を頼ってばかりいるのね.」
   "You _____ her, aren't you?"

Little Quiz

1. 次の face に関する表現は, どのような顔あるいは表情でしょうか, 絵で表してみましょう.

   a. an unpainted face

   b. a blank face

   c. a baby face

   d. a dark face

   e. a strong face

   f. a straight face

   g. a grim face

   h. an oily face

   i. a pouting face

   j. a long face

2. 日本の祭りの時の掛け声といえば, 神輿を担ぐ際の「ワッショイ」が一般的ですが, 地方の祭り（例えば阿波踊りやねぶた祭り）によっては独特な掛け声があります. その中から掛け声を一つ選び, その成り立ちをグループで調べて, 発表してみましょう.

Vocabulary Quiz

空所に入れるのに適した単語を，a～dの中から選び丸をつけましょう．

1. the _____ of the Olympic Games　　　　（オリンピック競技の呼び物）
   a. call　　　　b. calling　　　　c. highlight　　　　d. high five

2. My parents live close _____.　　　　（両親は近くに住んでいます）
   a. by　　　　b. to　　　　c. up　　　　d. on

3. _____ the plan　　　　（その計画を認可する）
   a. advocate　　b. approve　　　c. pursue　　　　d. favor

4. _____ a CD　　　　（CDを新発売する）
   a. sell　　　　b. lease　　　　c. sale　　　　d. release

5. caffeine-_____ instant coffee　　（カフェイン抜きのインスタントコーヒー）
   a. without　　b. no　　　　c. leaving　　　　d. free

6. _____ foods　　　　（発酵食品）
   a. fermented　　b. ferment　　c. fermentation　　d. fermentable

Grammar Check

1. X – free は「Xがない」を表す形容詞を作りますが,次の句はどのような意味でしょうか？
   pesticide-free organic vegetables
   additive-free food
   vehicle-free promenade

2. アメリカ英語とイギリス英語で，スペルが異なる場合があります．では，次の各組の単語
   の内，イギリス英語のスペルはどちらでしょうか？
   center – centre
   colour – color
   dialog – dialogue
   organize – organise
   programme – program
   gray – grey
   toward – towards
   defence – defense

Foreign tourists love Kyoto, and drinking tea in a quiet tearoom is the highlight of the Kyoto trip for many visitors. Some foreigners know that most tea grand masters live in Kyoto, so it feels like the centre of the tea world. When tourists to Kyoto sit in *seiza* as they drink *matcha* tea, many people mistakenly believe that they are drinking tea grown somewhere close by, like Uji.

Hoshino Sei Cha En has been changing tea history since 1987 when the Grand Master of the Edo Senke tea school approved the tea grown in Yame, Fukuoka Prefecture, as officially acceptable for the students of his tea school to use. In 1993 the Kyoto-based Grand Master of the Urasenke tea school also approved tea grown in Yame for official school use. A total of nine grand masters have approved eighteen different *matcha* teas, and the head priest of Shofukuji in Hakata has also chosen three varieties of *matcha* tea powder for use in his zen temple. When tourists drink tea in Kyoto, some of that tea comes from the Yame fields of Hoshino Sei Cha En.

Most foreigner tourists don't realize that tradition and innovation are two sides of the same coin. After being the first to break the tradition of 'Uji-cha is real tea' with its line of *matcha* tea, Hoshino Sei Cha En has released many new products. In 1992, the company released western style black tea, and high grade instant tea was introduced in 1998. In 2002 Hoshino Sei Cha En received the JAS Organic stamp of approval. The caffeine-free *ama cha* was sold from 2007. The new products for 2008 were Hoshi no *matcha* Au Lait and a lightly fermented oolong tea. But the big news in 2018 was the sale of a very delicious *matcha* chocolate!

注：**officially acceptable** 公式認可　JAS **Organic stamp of approval** 有機 JAS 規格

京都の外国人観光客の日本茶に対する印象は？

八女茶を知っていますか？

星野製茶園の製品は？

Based on the Passage, please choose the best answer.

1. What does the first paragraph say about tourists?
    A. All foreign tourists love the traditions of Kyoto.
    B. Some foreign tourists think Kyoto is in the middle of the map of Japan.
    C. Many Kyoto visitors do not understand how Kyoto traditions depend on things made a long away from Kyoto.
    D. Few foreign visitors master the art of drinking Kyoto tea.

2. What does the second paragraph say about Hoshino Sei Cha En?
    A. Hoshino Sei Cha En grows all the tea in Yame.
    B. More than ten Grand masters want their students to use Hoshino Sei Cha En tea.
    C. Real tea is grown in Uji, so tea school students cannot serve tea grown in Hoshino-mura.
    D. Despite being grown in Kyushu, the authentic taste of Kyoto includes Hoshino Sei Cha En tea.

3. What does the third paragraph say about the tradition of tea?
    A. The grand master schools of tea traditions are opposed to change.
    B. Most of the new tea products from the last thirty years all came from Uji.
    C. To be successful in the traditional world of tea, it is necessary to create something new.
    D. Although the origin of tea was a bitter medicine, the best-selling tea products these days are very sweet.

Dialogue

次の対話を聞いて，下線部を埋めてみよう.

Sky: If you are so bored with the trip so far, why don't you ₁_____ and go on the bungee jump tour tomorrow?

Clay: Apart from ₂_____ heights and not having enough money, ₃_____.

Sky: Listen, we can book you in online and I can ₄_____ my credit card.

Clay: OK ... Well, if you book for both of us, I will do it.

Sky: ₅_____ then! This is something we won't forget!

Based on the Dialogue, choose the best answer.

1. Who are the two people talking?
   A. Two people shopping together
   B. A supervisor and an employee
   C. Two people travelling together
   D. A travel agent and a tourist

2. What will the two people do tomorrow?
   A. Take part in bungee jumping
   B. Inspect bungee jumping
   C. Watch other people bungee jump
   D. Have no plan

Useful Expressions for Conversation

1. 承諾する：相手の申し出を受け入れる表現

   次の文の中で，相手の申し出を受け入れる表現はどれですか？
   a. That's a deal!
   b. Enough is enough!
   c. I bet!
   d. You bet!

2. 提案する：相手に提案する表現

   次の文の中で，提案を示す時に用いられる表現はどれですか？
   a. Why bother to study German at all?
   b. Why should I know?
   c. Why did she do it?
   d. Why don't we meet and discuss it?

以下の下線部に日本文の意味に合うように適切な語（句）を入れ, その後, ペアで読んでみましょう.

1. 「勇気を出して自分の間違いを認めるべきだよ.」

   "You just have to _____ and admit you were wrong."

   「頑張ってみるよ.」

   " I'll _____."

2. 「ニュース番組以外はテレビを見ないんだ.」

   "_____ the news, I don't watch TV."

   「えー, 僕もさ.」

   "Oh, _____ too."

1. 英語で tea と言えば, 通例「紅茶」を指しますが, 日本で飲める次の様々なお茶を英語で言ってみましょう.

a.	ウーロン茶	_____ tea
b.	緑茶	_____ tea
c.	玄米茶	_____ tea
d.	ジャスミン茶	_____ tea
e.	麦茶	_____ tea
f.	ハーブティー	_____ tea
g.	アイスティー	_____ tea
h.	濃いお茶	_____ tea
i.	薄いお茶	_____ tea
j.	入れたてのお茶	_____ tea

2. お茶を材料にした飲み物や食べ物の中で, あなたが好きなものを一つ選んで, そのイラストや画像を用いて, 英語で簡潔に紹介してみましょう.

Unit 5

Don't Know What You Got (Till It's Gone)

Vocabulary Quiz

空所に入れるのに適した単語を，a〜dの中から選び丸をつけましょう．

1. _____ at a person （人をじっと見る）
   a. see　　　　b. glimpse　　　　c. glance　　　　d. stare
2. have a long-_____ view （長期的な視点をもつ）
   a. time　　　b. term　　　　c. stay　　　　d. sighted
3. global _____ （地球温暖化）
   a. warm　　　b. warmer　　　c. warming　　　d. warmth
4. _____ order （秩序を回復させる）
   a. recover　　b. revive　　　c. regain　　　d. restore
5. be well _____ （しっかりと文書（音声・写真・映像）で記録されている）
   a. document　b. documenting　c. documented　d. documentary
6. full of _____ （栄養分たっぷりの）
   a. nutrients　b. nutrition　　c. nutritional　d. nutritious

Grammar Check

1. 英語では「見る」仕方によって，単語を使い分けます．次の「見方」を右の単語と結び付けてみましょう．

   こっそりと見る　　　　gaze
   熱心に見る　　　　　　glance
   じろじろ見る　　　　　glare
   ちらりと見る　　　　　stare
   ぎろりと見る　　　　　peep

2. be able to を過去時制で用いた場合，could とは少し意味が異なってきます．次の文には was（were）able to と could のいずれが入るでしょうか？

   She _____ climb the tree easily yesterday.
   She _____ climb trees easily when she was a child.
   We _____ only see the way when the moon was out.

Next time you take a holiday to Okinawa and are staring at that beautiful ocean, remember that those coral reefs do more than just protect our coasts from waves, storms, and floods. While the barriers of coral help prevent loss of life, property damage, and erosion, coral reefs also support people who work in tourism and fisheries. In terms of the long-term view, research scientists are studying how coral-reef plants and animals can be used in the medicines of the future to treat cancer and heart disease.

珊瑚礁の役割とは？

The coral reefs of Onnason, Okinawa Prefecture, are doing better than some other shorelines — coral reefs around the world are being damaged by pollution, blast fishing and ocean warming. In 2004, Team Tyura Sango, a partnership among local and national businesses, the Japanese government, and Japanese university researchers and their student volunteers, started to restore and protect the local reefs. The regular Facebook updates of Team Tyura Sango document how the underwater coral farming of volunteers, including growing corals in onshore nurseries and reattaching broken coral pieces, has restored many damaged reef sites.

珊瑚礁保護のためには？

All around the world, organizations like Team Tyura Sango are educating people to live in a way that increases the chances of our grandchildren being able to enjoy the economic, lifestyle and health benefits of stronger ecosystems in our oceans. Given that a coral reef ecosystem can be damaged by toxic poisons from oil and chemical spills, sediments produced by farming and cutting down forests, and nutrients that escape from failed septic systems, more attention to land and water management by citizens, business and government will help coral reefs to continue being a vital part of the ocean environment.

自然環境を保護するためには？

注：**erosion** 土壌の浸食　**tourism** 観光事業　**blast fishing** 爆発狩猟（ダイナマイト漁）　**onshore nurseries** 浜辺苗床・養サンゴ場　**toxic poisons** 有毒な毒　**chemical spills** 化学物質の流出　**sediments** 堆積物　**failed septic systems** 壊れた汚水処理タンク方式

Comprehension Questions

Based on the Passage, please choose the best answer.

1. What does the first paragraph say about the importance of coral reefs?

    A. Our coasts protect coral reefs from waves, storms, and floods.

    B. Coral reefs can be economically important only in the long term.

    C. Coral reefs have important short term and long-term benefits.

    D. Taking a holiday to Okinawa will help cure your heart disease.

2. What does the second paragraph say about overcoming the difficulties of protecting local reefs?

    A. More dynamite is the fastest solution to the problem of restoring local reefs.

    B. Facebook sites show how ocean warming restores damaged reefs.

    C. Raising volunteers in nurseries limits pollution damage.

    D. One key action is linking people from business, government and universities.

3. What does the third paragraph say about changing how society values the environment?

    A. All of the following answers are correct.

    B. Changing how we live now can have a positive impact on the long-term health of coral reefs.

    C. How forests are managed is important for coral reefs.

    D. As citizens, business and government are part of the problem, they can work together to be part of the answer of how to protect the environment for future generations.

Dialogue

次の対話を聞いて，下線部を埋めてみよう．

Ruby: So when the boat starts moving, I start running, and then I get lifted. I float up ₁_____ and we do a ₂_____ lap of the island and then I get softly dropped into the shallow water near the beach ₃_____, right?

Kai: Uh-huh.

Ruby: ₄_____, why has the shark patrol boat been doing those ₅_____ inside the lagoon for the last fifteen minutes?

Kai: Well ... let's see. I don't really know ...

23

Based on the Dialogue, choose the best answer.

1. What is Ruby going to do?
   A. Windsurf
   B. Water-ski
   C. Parasail
   D. Sky dive

2. In the last line of the dialogue, why does Kai refuse to give a direct answer?
   A. Because Kai doesn't understand the question of Ruby.
   B. Because Kai doesn't like Ruby.
   C. Because Kai knows nothing at all.
   D. Because Kai understands that there is a shark in the water.

Useful Expressions for Conversation

1. つなぎ：つなぎを表す表現

   次の文の下線部の中で，つなぎを表す表現はどれですか？
   a. <u>Let's see</u> ... What was the girl's name?
   b. <u>Let me see</u> your passport.
   c. "I bought a new bike." "Really? <u>Let's see</u>."
   d. <u>Let me see</u> ... Is Professor Tanaka's lecture canceled today?

2. 新たな話題の導入：前に述べたことと関連する新たな話題を導入する表現

   次の文の下線部の中で，新たな話題を導入する際に用いられる表現はどれですか？
   a. <u>By the way</u>, have you seen Jenny recently?
   b. We will fly to Hawaii <u>by way of</u> Seoul.
   c. <u>Either way</u>, I don't like her.
   d. <u>In a way</u>, we are responsible for it.

Practical Use

以下の下線部に日本文の意味に合うように適切な語（句）を入れ，その後，ペアで読んでみましょう。

1. 「今日の小テストはどうだった？」

"How did you do on the quiz today?"

「えっとー，きっと満点をとれたと思う．」
"_____ ... I'm sure I got 100 percent."

2. 「ところで，賛成の人は挙手してください．」
"_____, all（those）_____, raise your hand."

「賛成！」
"Yes / Aye!"

Little Quiz

1. アメリカで holiday と言えば，日曜日のことは指さず祝日のことですが，日本の祝日とは異なり，日にちではなく曜日で指定されていることの方が多いという特徴があります．では以下の祝日はどういうもので，いつでしょうか，調べて発表してみましょう．

   a. New Year's Day
   b. Martin Luther King Day
   c. Independence Day
   d. Labor Day
   e. Thanksgiving Day
   f. Columbus Day
   g. Christmas Day

2. オーストラリアの祝祭日は，国が定めたもの（以下の a ～ d）と州ごとに定めたもの（e ～ g）があります．ではその祝祭日はどういうもので，いつでしょうか，調べて発表してみましょう．

   a. Australia Day
   b. Boxing Day
   c. Good Friday
   d. Easter Monday
   e. Melbourne Cup Day（Victoria）
   f. Bank Holiday（New South Wales）
   g. King Island Show（Tasmania）

Vocabulary Quiz

空所に入れるのに適した単語を，a～dの中から選び丸をつけましょう．

1. live _____ oneself　　　　　　　　　　（一人で（単身で）暮らす）
   a. by　　　　b. for　　　　c. in　　　　d. to

2. a _____ student　　　　　　　　　　（同級生）
   a. classmate　b. same　　c. fellow　　d. grade

3. a _____ teacher　　　　　　　　　　（退職した先生）
   a. retirement　b. retire　　c. retiring　　d. retired

4. _____ one's goal　　　　　　　　　　（目標を達成する）
   a. achieve　　b. define　　c. establish　　d. make

5. job _____　　　　　　　　　　（仕事探し，求職）
   a. sharing　　b. hunting　　c. opening　　d. hopping

6. _____ events　　　　　　　　　　（イベントを企画する）
   a. make　　　b. mark　　　c. plane　　　d. organize

Grammar Check

1. 「使いやすいパソコンが欲しい」を英語で言う時，下線部に入るのは，to use と using のいずれが適格ですか？

   I want a computer that is easy _____.

2. 英米人のお宅におじゃまして，「もう暗くなったので，おいとましなければなりません」と言いたい場合，相手の気分を害さないようにするには，下線部に must と have to のどちらを入れるのが適切ですか？

   "It's getting dark. So I _____ leave now."

Take a quick look around your classroom. You will see students who live with their family, students who live together in dormitories, and students who live by themselves. Now look at the students who live by themselves and then ask how many of these students come to class without cooking themselves breakfast. Maybe you will be surprised by how many of your fellow students try to start studying without eating the most important meal of the day.

今日は大学に来る前に朝食を食べましたか？

Many students sometimes skip breakfast or might just get some sugary junk food from a convenience store but students who live by themselves are the group that most regularly misses breakfast. Nutrition students from Shikoku established Nuways to help educate fellow students and older community members about the importance of food in creating a healthy lifestyle. By sharing what they have learned in their classrooms with retired people outside the university, members of Nuways are learning how to work effectively in society as they do their volunteer activities.

四国の Nuways という団体を知っていますか？

The success of Nuways is driven by students who know how to achieve their goals by connecting studying, learning and teaching. These students understand that volunteer activities are an important part of job hunting. They have to plan and organize events, choosing locations that are easy for town people to find, and match the contents of their workshops to the interests of the people who come to learn about improving their life through food. These skills are important for young people trying to find their first job, but, in the short term, teaching other people what they have learned in class is the best way to get ready for the year-end exams!

Nuways の活動を通して得られたスキルとは？

注：**junk food** ジャンクフード（カロリーは高いが栄養に欠けるスナック菓子）
　　nutrition students 栄養学を学ぶ学生

Comprehension Questions

Based on the Passage, please choose the best answer.

1. What does the first paragraph say about students?
    A. Nutrition is the foundation for educational success.
    B. Students can be divided into groups based on calorie intake.
    C. The eating habits of students are influenced by how they live.
    D. It is surprising how many students understand the importance of balancing a healthy diet with enough exercise.

2. What does the second paragraph say about students?
    A. Shy retiring students are happy to eat breakfast outside a convenience store.
    B. Students who live in dormitories miss having breakfast with their families.
    C. Educated students balance healthy breakfasts with junk food snacks.
    D. Students from Shikoku apply their classroom study of nutrition to help change how people outside the university live.

3. What does the third paragraph say about students changing society?
    A. All of the following.
    B. When students connect studying and learning by teaching what they have studied, they will have an advantage in the job hunting market.
    C. To work effectively, students must have an idea that catches the attention of people who want to change their lives.
    D. If students chose a hard-to-find place to share that idea, the chances of success will be reduced.

Dialogue   13

次の対話を聞いて，下線部を埋めてみよう．

Lani: I am so sorry that you cannot ₁_____.

Drake: If the airplane had not sent my suitcase to ₂_____, I would have been in ₃_____ on Christmas Eve, ready to be Santa Claus for my kids.

Lani: The check-in-staff made a ₄_____ mistake. As much as I would love to able to offer you an upgrade to business class, the best we can do make sure you have a row of empty seats in ₅_____.

Drake: All right then ... I guess I am lucky that you can get me on the next plane at this time of year.

TOEIC Challenge

Based on the Dialogue, choose the best answer.

1. Where does Lani work?
   - A. In Austria
   - B. In Australia
   - C. At a control tower
   - D. At an airline company

2. What will Drake do next?
   - A. Fly to Austria in economy class
   - B. Fly to Austria in business class
   - C. Fly to Australia in economy class
   - D. Fly to Australia in business class

Useful Expressions for Conversation

1. 謝罪する：謝罪の際に用いられる表現

   次の文の中で，自分が謝罪する際に用いられる表現はどれですか？
   - a. I accept your apology.
   - b. Please accept our apologies for causing such inconvenience.
   - c. I'm sorry I didn't call you earlier.
   - d. Sorry to hear that.

2. 譲歩を表す表現

   次の文の中で，譲歩を示す時に用いられる表現はどれですか？
   - a. As much as he wanted to stay at the party, he had to leave.
   - b. Much as I like Bill, I wouldn't want to take a trip with him.
   - c. Drink as much coffee as you like.
   - d. I love baseball as much as soccer.

以下の下線部に日本文の意味に合うように適切な語（句）を入れ，その後，ペアで読んでみましょう．

1. 「先日は本当にすまなかった．」

   "I am really _____ the other day."

   「どういたしまして．」

   "_____."

2. 「行きたいのはやまやまだが，野暮用でちょっと手が離せないんだ．」

   "_____ I'd like to go, I'm busy right now on some minor business."

   「お気の毒さま！」

   "Oh, I'm _____ that."

   (= That's too bad.)

Little Quiz

1. 「朝食」のことを英語で breakfast と言う理由を知っていますか？（ヒント：break + fast）

2. 海外のホテルで提供される「朝食」には，以下のようなタイプがあります．自分の好きなタイプを，イラストあるいは画像を用いて，説明してみましょう．

   a. Continental breakfast
   b. American breakfast
   c. English breakfast
   d. Breakfast buffet
   e. Vegan keto breakfast

Vocabulary Quiz

空所に入れるのに適した単語を，a ～ d の中から選び丸をつけましょう．

1. get caught _____ in a crime　　　　　　（犯罪に巻き込まれる）

    a. up　　　　　b. on　　　　　c. down　　　　d. under

2. a _____ of questions　　　　　　　　（多くの質問）

    a. bunt　　　　b. bunch　　　　c. bench　　　d. bend

3. _____ blood　　　　　　　　　　　（献血する）

    a. cough　　　b. draw　　　　c. donate　　　d. type

4. _____ statistics　　　　　　　　　（統計を集める）

    a. examine　　b. study　　　c. tabulate　　d. gather

5. a _____ story　　　　　　　　　　（滑稽な話）

    a. fan　　　　b. fancy　　　c. funny　　　d. funnily

6. combine two parties _____ one　　（二つの党を結合して一つの党にする）

    a. into　　　　b. in　　　　　c. to　　　　　d. for

Grammar Check

1. 次の返答の下線部に入る「たぶん」の英訳としては，probably, maybe, possibly のいずれが適切でしょうか？

    A：When will you be back?

    B：_____ next Monday, but I'm not sure.

2. 次の西暦を読んでみましょう．

    804, 1994, 2000, 2009, 2024

Maybe it all started with an unpleasant shock, like someone from your class getting caught up in a car accident and having to be taken to hospital. When a bunch of friends visit the hospital once things settle down, someone sees a poster there asking people to donate blood. Or maybe it was something simpler and quieter, and closer to home. Maybe someone in your class had a mother who was a doctor or worked in a hospital and that person knew that Japanese hospitals needed more volunteers to supply blood as preparation for the chaos of natural disasters.

輸血の大切さを知ると
は？

When the Sapporo student members of Tomato Club looked at blood donation statistics, they saw four important points. In Japan, men donate 70% and women give only 30% of blood donations. Although men in their forties make up 20% of all Japanese donations, men in their twenties give only 10%. Most importantly, blood donations have been falling since 2012 when more than 2,000,000 liters of blood were collected. Inside Japan, more than 40% of blood donations are made at bloodmobiles, like the ones that make regular visits to your university campus.

献血者を増やすには？

Outside of Japan there are plenty of funny slogans asking for blood donations. 'Don't let mosquitoes get your blood first.' 'I gave my blood for cookies!' 'You are somebody's type, please donate.' 'Starve a vampire. Give blood.' Some slogans make different appeals: 'Recycle yourself. Donate.' Other play with language. 'Share a little, care a little, donate blood.' 'Spend 30 minutes, save three lives.' In America, even the names of the volunteer groups play with language by combining two words as one: BloodCare, BloodSource, LifeBlood, OneBlood. However, the soft and friendly feeling of Tomato Club seems to be helping the Sapporo students who are working to increase volunteer donations in Hokkaido: in 2013, student age donations by women were more than double those of men!

献血者を増やす海外の方
法とは？

Comprehension Questions

Based on the Passage, please choose the best answer.

1. What does the first paragraph say about how people learn the importance of blood donation?
   A. Being lectured by a doctor after causing a traffic accident.
   B. Being models for the poster used in a blood drive.
   C. Getting caught up in the problems caused by an earthquake.
   D. It might be a sudden event, a quick look at a poster, or being told by someone with a connection to a hospital.

2. What does the second paragraph say about the best way to increase blood donations in Japan?
   A. Ask men in their twenties to double their efforts.
   B. Ask women of all ages to double their efforts.
   C. Reduce the number of bloodmobiles so more blood is donated at hospitals.
   D. None of the above.

3. What does the third paragraph say about how English is used to increase blood donations outside Japan?
   A. Some slogans use rhyme.
   B. Some slogans use opposing verbs.
   C. Some slogans mash words together.
   D. The first two of the above answers are correct.

Dialogue

次の対話を聞いて，下線部を埋めてみよう．

Poppy: ₁＿＿＿＿＿＿ your eyes.

Brad: What is this, fourth grade?

Poppy: We lost ₂＿＿＿＿＿ in the capsize. You should look ₃＿＿＿＿＿.

Brad: Would it ₄＿＿＿＿＿ if I put some rope ₅＿＿＿＿＿ my mouth?

Poppy: Just use two hands to hang onto the rope and try not move too much ...

TOEIC Challenge

Based on the Dialogue, choose the best answer.

1. Who is Poppy?

A. A doctor

B. A patient

C. A captain

D. A sailor

2. What will Brad do next?

    A. Bite the rope

    B. Bite the bullet

    C. Bite his nails

    D. Bite his lip

Useful Expressions for Conversation

1. 助言する：助言の際に用いられる表現.

   次の文の中で，助言する際に用いられる表現はどれですか？

   a. You should take your umbrella in case it rains.

   b. You should have seen the movie.

   c. She should have arrived there by now.

   d. It is surprising that you should not know it.

2. 指示する：相手に指示する表現

   次の文の中で，相手への指示を表す表現はどれですか？

   a. Attention, please!

   b. Heat a frying pan and melt the butter.

   c. Watch out.

   d. Wait a minute.

Practical Use

以下の下線部に日本文の意味に合うように適切な語（句）を入れ，その後,ペアで読んでみましょう.

1. 「今日，天気はぐずつくみたいね.」

   "The weather will _____ today."

   「折り畳み傘を持っていくといいよ.」

   "You _____ your folding umbrella."

2. 「血圧を測りますね. 深呼吸をしてください.」

"I'll check your blood pressure. _____ a deep breath!"

「はい. 血圧は高い方です.」

"Sure. I have _____ blood pressure."

Little Quiz

1. 二つの語を組み合わせて一つの語にする場合, 二つの語の一部をつなげて一つの語にすることは混成（blending）と呼ばれます. たとえば, brunch は breakfast と lunch から作られた混成語（blend）です. では, 次の混成語はどういう二つの語から作られたのでしょうか？

    a.   informercial （生放送のコマーシャル）

    b.   telethon   （基金募集のための長時間テレビ）

    c.   anklet   （アンクレット）

    d.   cineplex   （スクリーンのたくさんある映画館）

    e.   cosplay   （コスプレ）

    f.   spork   （先割れスプーン）

    g.   internet   （インターネット）

    h.   netiquette   （ネチケット）

    i.   pixel   （ピクセル）

    j.   emoticon   （顔文字）

2. 上記の混成語は日本語の中にもあります. 例えば, 天ぷら＋どんぶり＞天丼, グラビア＋アイドル＞グラドル, 自動車＋学校＞車校, 等があります. 他にも日本語の混成語の例を挙げ, 英語の混成語のタイプと比較して, その構成に相違があるのかを調べて発表してみましょう.

Unit 8 Justice

Vocabulary Quiz

空所に入れるのに適した単語を，a～d の中から選び丸をつけましょう.

1. a _____ TV   （白黒テレビ）
   a. black and white   b. white and black   c. color   d. monochromatic

2. _____ a difference   （差を生じる）
   a. see   b. feel   c. distinguish   d. make

3. a _____ decision   （公平な決定）
   a. fare   b. fair   c. fear   d. fore

4. the _____ of a company   （会社の組織）
   a. organization   b. organizational   c. organize   d. organizer

5. _____ problems   （問題に直面する）
   a. head   b. face   c. hand   d. eye

6. _____ economic growth   （維持できる経済成長）
   a. sustain   b. sustained   c. sustaining   d. sustainable

Grammar Check

1. 次の文において all が修飾しているのは，my friends と these questions のいずれですか？

   a. *All* my friends must answer these questions.
   b. My friends must *all* answer these questions.
   c. My friends must answer *all* these questions.

2. 次の文の下線部の「たとえば」を表す表現として，for example と such as のいずれが適切ですか？

   The Romance languages, _____ French, Italian, and Spanish, are derived from Latin.

In those old black-and-white cowboy movies, when a group of American men ride their horses out of town, that group is called a posse. As this posse leaves the town to solve a problem in the name of justice, the men usually all have guns and sometimes a few of them are drunk. In modern Japan, however, Posse has a much more peaceful way of solving problems.

正義とは？

Posse is one of many groups of young people that are making a difference in Japan. Living here is becoming easier because student groups are working as volunteers outside university to make life fair for everyone. For example, Posse has helped people who cannot find a job, who are being treated unfairly at work and those who don't have enough money to eat. Last year posse helped about 3,000 people.

生活は公平？

Since 2006, Posse has grown to be an organization of about 50 members and most of these people are still younger than thirty. The Setagaya City magazine *Job Handbook for Young People* recommended that new workers facing any labor problems should contact Posse. Posse and other groups that directly help people-in-need can give us all hope for more equality in a friendlier Japan. These groups are also learning how to improve the future of Japanese society: they use their real world research of trying to fix actual problems to make suggestions for social politics that support more sustainable lifestyles and culture.

日本の社会を変える？

注：**posse** 民警団　**in the name of ~** 　の名目で，~の名において

Based on the Passage, please choose the best answer.

1. What does the first paragraph say about justice?

    A. The best recipe for justice is guns, a group of men, and some alcohol.

    B. The most peaceful way to fix a problem is to give guns to angry people.

    C. Justice does not have to be violent.

    D. Time and place don't change justice: it is always the same everywhere.

2. What does the second paragraph say about life being fair?

    A. Blond hair and fair skin make it easier to live in Japan.

    B. It is not fair that Japanese students cannot find jobs in Japan.

    C. Last year, three thousand people didn't have enough money to eat.

    D. Life is not fair to everyone and volunteering to help other people is good.

3. What does the third paragraph say about students changing society?

    A. The best social policies are made by testing how research can help people in need.

    B. Students are too young to be trusted to change society.

    C. Setagaya City is proud of being friendlier to homeless people.

    D. Changing society is too difficult for people under thirty.

Dialogue

次の対話を聞いて，下線部を埋めてみよう．

Rudy: Listen your English is fine.

Ren: It was fine ₁_____ I came back from that year of study in Newcastle. But I haven't really spoken to anyone ₂_____. And that was two years back …

Rudy: ₃_____ you forgetting something? When the rugby team from Newcastle University came here last year, you were the only one who could understand ₄_____!

Ren: Oh yeah, that was a fun night. I really should have gone out drinking with them after the game. It would have been a pretty wild night, ₅_____?

TOEIC Challenge

Based on the Dialogue, choose the best answer.

1. When did Rudy return from study abroad?

A. Last year

B. Two years ago

C. Three years ago

D. Four years ago

2. Who went out drinking with the rugby team from Newcastle last year?

A. Ren

B. Rudy and Ren

C. Someone and Ren

D. No one

Useful Expressions for Conversation

1. 思い起こさせる表現：否定疑問文

肯定疑問文（a）が中立的に Yes か No の答えを求めるのに対して，否定疑問文（b）は
どのような状況で用いられるでしょうか？

a. Do you remember the day we first met?

b. Don't you remember the day we first met?

2. 否定疑問文に対する応答
次の否定疑問文（上の 1b）に対する返答としては，次の a ～ d のいずれが適切でしょうか？

Don't you remember the day we first met?（初めて会った日のこと，覚えてないの？）

a. Yes, I do.　　　　（はい，覚えている．）

b. Yes, I don't.　　　（はい，覚えていない．）

c. No, I do.　　　　（いいえ，覚えている．）

d. No, I don't.　　　（いいえ，覚えていない．）

Practical Use

以下の下線部に日本文の意味に合うように適切な語（句）を入れ，その後，ペアで読んでみましょ
う．

1. 「じっとしていられないの？写真を撮りますよ.」

   "Can't you _____ ? I'm going to take a picture."

   「わかりました.」

"All right."

2. 「あなたも私と意見が一緒でしょう？」
"You _____?"

「さあ，私にはちょっとわかりません．彼の言うこともももっともだとは思うけど．」
"Well, I don't know. _____ to me too."

Little Quiz

1. 二つの語を and で並列する場合，日本語と英語で，その順序が同じであったり，異なったりします．次の日本語は英語ではどういう順序になるでしょうか？

白黒映画 ［black/white］	a _____ {film / movie}
白黒写真	a _____ photograph
紅白の餅 ［red/white］	_____ rice cakes
行き来 ［go/come］	_____
時々（occasionally）［then/now］	I go for a drink _____.（時々飲みに出かけます）
時々・断続的に ［on/off］	It rained _____ yesterday.（昨日は雨が降ったりやんだりした）
すぐその場で ［then/there］	I felt _____ that she was the one for me.（彼女が運命の人だとすぐその場で感じた）

2. 日本語と英語の色彩表現に関して，共通の色を用いた表現と異なる色を用いた表現を調べて，発表してみましょう．例：赤信号：red light, 青信号：*green* light, 黄信号：yellow light

Life before Special Adoption

Vocabulary Quiz

空所に入れるのに適した単語を，a～dの中から選び丸をつけましょう．

1. _____ people from starvation　　　　（人々を飢えから救う）
   a. relieve　　　b. aid　　　c. help　　　d. save

2. _____ evidence　　　　（確たる証拠）
   a. hard　　　b. soft　　　c. convinced　　　d. concrete

3. _____ a person as a murderer　　　　（殺人犯として逮捕する）
   a. attract　　　b. arrest　　　c. arrestment　　　d. catch

4. look _____ children　　　　（子供たちの世話をする）
   a. before　　　b. after　　　c. through　　　d. over

5. _____ one's children carefully　　　　（自分の子供たちを慎重に育てる）
   a. arise　　　b. rise　　　c. raise　　　d. bring

6. place first _____ on ～　　　　（～を最優先する）
   a. prior　　　b. priory　　　c. priority　　　d. prioritize

Grammar Check

1. 次の文において，「彼女が運試しに実際に石を持ち上げようとしたが，できなかった」場合，いずれの表現が適格でしょうか？

   a. She tried to lift the stone just to try her luck, but she couldn't.
   b. She tried lifting the stone just to try her luck, but she couldn't.

2. more than ten people は，厳密には「10 人以上」それとも「11 人以上」のいずれを表しますか？

When the most famous graduate of Sasebo-kita High School in Nagasaki Prefecture, Murakami Ryu, won the Third Noma Bungei Shinjin Prize for his *Coin Locker Babies* novel in 1981 (one year before the other Murakami ...), most people in Japan had not thought too much about having to make a choice between abortion and adoption. Although Germany tried having a 'baby post' system in 1999, it was not until May 2007 when Japan's first baby hatch was established by Jikei Hospital in Kumamoto.

1982 年に村上という名前で思い浮かぶのは？

In 2009 the German Ethics Council said there was no hard evidence that the baby hatch system was actually saving the lives of babies. In France women can safely give birth in a hospital without telling anyone their names, so the baby hatch system is not necessary there. In Japan, however, police were arresting women because they abandoned or killed their newborn babies after giving birth without going to hospital.

日本で母親が新生児を捨てると？

Parents who felt it was impossible for them to look after their children left 130 children at the Jikei Hospital baby hatch in the ten years since 2007. Despite criticism that the baby hatch system prevents children from knowing their biological parents, little more than 30% of the women who left their babies at Jikei Hospital are from Kyushu, and the remainder travel from Honshu. When some parents who used the baby system were asked why they could not keep their babies, they were given a choice of five answers: being single (28 people), concerns about reputation or relatives complaining about listing the newborn baby in the family register (21 people), not having enough money to raise the child (17 people), illicit sexual relations (14 people), strong opposition from parents (10 people). After the April 14 2016 Kumamoto earthquake, when Jikei Hospital appealed for food assistance before sharing food with local evacuation centers and cooking meals for more than 450 people, everyone understood what the hospital was doing: saving lives is always the top priority.

赤ちゃんポストを利用する理由は？

注：**abortion**　妊娠中絶　　**adoption**　養子縁組　　**baby hatch**　赤ちゃんポスト
biological parents　実の親　　**family register**　戸籍謄本
illicit sexual relations　不倫関係

Comprehension Questions

Based on the Passage, please choose the best answer.

1. In the first paragraph, who is the other Murakami?
    A. Artist Murakami Takashi.
    B. Children's doctor Murakami Hitoshi.
    C. Writer Murakami Momoko.
    D. Author Murakami Haruki.

2. What does the second paragraph say about Japanese law?
    A. It is an offence to deliver a baby without going to a hospital.
    B. It is not against the law to deliver a baby without going to a hospital.
    C. Both of the above answers are correct.
    D. Answers A and B are both incorrect.

3. What does the third paragraph say about why people use the baby hatch system?
    A. Getting pregnant from an affair is a more common reason than being poor.
    B. The lack of parental support is a more common reason than not being married.
    C. Both of the above answers are correct.
    D. Answers A and B are both incorrect.

Dialogue

次の対話を聞いて，下線部を埋めてみよう．

Felix: I'm sorry, but I couldn't hear you ₁_____. Bad reception out here, I guess. Could you say that again please?

Bruno: One day and three hundred dollars.

Felix: Seriously? One day and three hundred dollars just to ₂_____? Are you kidding me?

Bruno: Listen, it's the night before Christmas, the next place for repairs is two hundred kilometers away, and the wife of the mechanic is very pregnant, ₃_____
...

Felix: Yeah, OK, I ₄_____. It sounds tough your end. Sorry but I have to get home by tomorrow night, so how about you let the mechanic stay at home, I leave the rental car here, and you get someone to drive me to the airport now for ₅_____?

Bruno: One family man to another, merry Christmas!

TOEIC Challenge

Based on the Dialogue, choose the best answer.

1. Where are Felix and Bruno?
   A. An auto repair shop
   B. A cake shop
   C. A hospital
   D. A car-rental agency

2. What will Bruno do next?
   A. Buy a Christmas cake
   B. Take the mechanic's wife to the hospital
   C. Have another mechanic take Felix to the airport
   D. Do nothing

Useful Expressions for Conversation

1. 聞き返し：相手の言ったことを聞き返す際の表現

   次の文の中で，相手の言ったことを聞き返す時の表現はどれですか？
   a. Come again?
   b. Could you say that again?
   c. I beg your pardon?
   d. Sorry?

2. 理解：相手の言ったことを理解したことを示す表現

   次の文の中で，相手の言ったことが理解できたことを示す表現はどれですか？
   a. Now I get it.
   b. Get it?
   c. I know what.
   d. That makes sense.

Practical Use

以下の下線部に日本文の意味に合うように適切な語（句）を入れ，その後，ペアで読んでみましょう．

1. 「声が小さくてよく聞き取れませんでした．もう一度言ってもらえませんか？」
   "You spoke too softly, so I couldn't really hear you very well.
   _____?"

   「了解です.」
   "O.K."

2. 「これはここだけの話だよ．わかった？」
   "This is just between _____. _____ ?"

   「大丈夫，誰にも言わないよ.」
   "Don't worry. I won't _____."

Little Quiz

1. イギリスの通貨単位は，penny と pound であるのに対し，アメリカ，カナダ，オーストラリアの通貨単位は，cent と dollar です．penny と cent は，それぞれ pound と dollar の 100 分の 1 です．アメリカの紙幣には，日本の紙幣同様，肖像が印刷されていますが，誰の肖像かを調べて，紙幣のデザインのイラストを描いて発表してみましょう．

   a. 1 ドル紙幣
   b. 2 ドル紙幣
   c. 5 ドル紙幣
   d. 10 ドル紙幣
   e. 20 ドル紙幣
   f. 50 ドル紙幣
   g. 100 ドル紙幣

2. 紙幣の肖像に選ばれる人物に関して，日本と外国とではどのような相違があるのかを調べて発表してみましょう．

Unit 10

You squeeze oranges, I throw tomatoes

Vocabulary Quiz

空所に入れるのに適した単語を，a～dの中から選び丸をつけましょう．

1. be _____ chaos （混沌としている，混乱している）
   a. at   b. on   c. in   d. into

2. a street _____ （露店）
   a. stole   b. stall   c. stool   d. steel

3. _____ nuclear weapons （核兵器を禁止する）
   a. pan   b. tan   c. fan   d. ban

4. _____ the rival （ライバルを打ち負かす）
   a. beat   b. strike   c. pat   d. slap

5. a _____ of knowledge （ちょっとした知識）
   a. pet   b. bet   c. bit   d. pit

6. childish _____ （子供っぽいいたずら）
   a. harm   b. damage   c. violence   d. mischief

Grammar Check

1. plan, decide の後ろに続くのは，それぞれ to+ 動詞と動詞 -ing のいずれでしょうか？

   I plan ｛to visit / visiting｝Boston next month.
   I decided not ｛to use / using｝my smartphone during a meal.

2. 次の文の next の前には the が必要ですか，それとも不要ですか？

   See you _____ next week. （また来週！）
   I saw you _____ next week. （その翌週に君に会った．）

Valencia is famous for Spanish oranges and a first-rate football team in Liga Espanol. Less than 40 kilometers west of Valencia is Buñol, a town that is becoming famous for its tomato food-fight festival. The beginnings of the La Tomatina festival was in the last year of World War II when some young people somehow started a food fight among themselves on the day of the local parade. They had so much fun on the last Wednesday of August 1945 that they planned to do it again the next year.

It seems that when these young people decided to suddenly appear in the 1945 music parade, they made some of the older players angry. In the chaos of the disagreement, a local vegetable stall was destroyed when the fruit and vegetables were thrown by the angry crowd. The next year those youngsters brought their own vegetables from home and enjoyed another food fight, despite getting some polite attention from the police. When they repeated their actions the following year, being arrested looked like part of their fun.

Police banned the food fight in the 1950s until a widespread protest in 1957. Musicians from the regular music parade played funeral music as a coffin holding a huge tomato was carried through the Buñol town square. The local politicians realized that they could not beat the support for the tomato food fight. The local media began promoting the festival, and the police made rules for the food fight. In 2002, something that began as a bit of mischief among young friends more than 50 years ago was declared a festival of International Tourism Interest of Spain.

注：**stall** 屋台　　**funeral music** 葬儀のエレジー　　**coffin** 棺桶

スペインのLa Tomatina（ラ・トマティーナ）festival を知っていますか？

若者が逮捕されたのはいつ？

フードファイトの伝統は？

Based on the Passage, please choose the best answer.

1. What does the first paragraph say about Spain in the last years of World War II?
   A. The tomatoes of Valencia were an important part of Liga Espanol soccer celebrations.
   B. Liga Espanol fans organized the La Tomatina festival.
   C. The end of the war was the beginnings of the La Tomatina festival.
   D. To train for the La Tomatina festival, Valencia soccer players ran 40 kilometers a week.

2. What does the second paragraph say about the arrest of the young people who started the food fights?
   A. Those young people were arrested in 1945.
   B. Those young people were arrested in 1946.
   C. Those young people were arrested in 1947.
   D. Police arrested those young people to protect them from the angry old musicians.

3. What does the third paragraph say about this food fight tradition?
   A. All of the following are incorrect.
   B. When the police band played traditional protest music, popular support for the food fight died.
   C. Once the fun and freedom of the food fight was controlled by rules, none of the local politicians were safe.
   D. An innocent beginning, helpful media coverage and endorsement by the national government were key moments in establishing this tradition.

Dialogue

次の対話を聞いて，下線部を埋めてみよう．

Hugo: It looks like fun, speeding ₁_____ and then suddenly jumping up into the sky before landing gently back on the water. ₂_____ if I could have a quick try before the end of my holiday.

Kip: ₃_____ is dangerous and this is one water sport you cannot learn in one sunny afternoon. In this school, we always spend the first day practicing on ₄_____.

Hugo: You know that I have been surfing for forty years, and windsurfing for fifteen, right? How about we skip the lesson that takes place on dry land and you let me go in the water with the smallest kite when the wind is not strong?

Kip:　Safety never takes a holiday.

Hugo:　I am going to interpret that as a ₅_____ ...

TOEIC Challenge

Based on the Dialogue, choose the best answer.

1. Who is Kip?
   A.　An instructor at a kitesurfing school
   B.　A student at a kitesurfing school
   C.　A visitor at a kitesurfing school
   D.　An amateur kitesurfer

2. What kind of lesson will Hugo practice first?
   A.　Practice windsurfing
   B.　Practice kitesurfing on the water
   C.　Practice kitesurfing on dry land
   D.　Practice swimming

Useful Expressions for Conversation

1. 依頼・申し出：丁寧な依頼や申し出の表現

   丁寧な依頼や申し出を表す場合，次の文のいずれが適切ですか？
   a.　Send it to me by the day after tomorrow.
   b.　Please send it to me by the day after tomorrow.
   c.　Will you send it to me by the day after tomorrow?
   d.　It would be great if you could send it to me by the day after tomorrow.

2. 提案する：相手に提案する表現

   次の文の中で，提案を示す時に用いられる表現はどれですか？
   a.　How come it happened?
   b.　How's that again?
   c.　How about meeting on Friday?
   d.　How could it happen?

Practical Use

以下の下線部に日本文の意味に合うように適切な語（句）を入れ，その後，ペアで読んでみましょう．

1. 「申込用紙を明日までに送っていただけると助かります．」
   "_____ if you could send me an application form by tomorrow."

   「かしこまりました．」
   "Certainly, sir."

2. 「来年ワーキングホリデイを利用しようかなと考えているんだけど．」
   "I'm thinking of _____ a working holiday."

   「鈴木教授に相談に行ったらどうかな？」
   "_____ with Professor Suzuki?"

Little Quiz

1. アメリカのお祭りには日本人に馴染み深いものからそうではないものまで，また定休日になっているものからそうではないものまでいろいろあります．次のお祭りはいつどのように行われるか，また法定休日になっているかどうか調べて発表してみましょう．

   a. Memorial Day
   b. Independence Day
   c. Labor Day
   d. Halloween
   e. Thanksgiving Day

2. 日本全国には，一年を通して多くのお祭りが開催されています．皆さんの地元にもいくつかのお祭りが開かれていることでしょう．そこで，自分の地元のお祭りを，簡潔に英語で紹介してみましょう．

Unit 11

Once upon a time ... And everyone lived happily ever after

Vocabulary Quiz

空所に入れるのに適した単語を，a 〜 d の中から選び丸をつけましょう.

1. _____ counties   （発展途上国）
   a. develop   b. developing   c. developed   d. developmental

2. _____ donations   （寄付を集める）
   a. recruit   b. raise   c. rise   d. collect

3. be full of _____   （やる気満々である）
   a. motivate   b. motivated   c. motivation   d. motivational

4. social _____   （社会的交流）
   a. interact   b. interaction   c. interactive   d. interactively

5. _____ one's dream   （夢の実現を目指す）
   a. chase   b. relate   c. dream   d. confide

6. the company's _____   （会社の収益）
   a. earn   b. earned   c. earnest   d. earnings

Grammar Check

1. 次の名詞の中で，数えられる用法と数えられない用法の両方あるものはどれでしょう？

   advice, direction, information, instruction, knowledge

2. 次の eel （ウナギ）はそれぞれ丸ごと一匹のウナギとウナギの一部のいずれを指していますか？
   a. I saw an eel in the river.
   b. I'd really like a bowl of eel and rice, please.

Once upon a time, in a university just like the one where you study, there was a group of student volunteers who wanted to change the world. As students, they all agreed that children in a developing country like Laos could have a better life if an education support project gave them what they needed to begin study. These Japanese university students made a non-profit organization but still needed online donations to turn their idea into concrete actions. Once they built a website, the simple donation form meant people could easily donate money with a couple of clicks. It was perfect: the money came when needed, the students got to help children in the developing country of Laos, and they changed the world one village at a time. Everyone lived happily ever after. (If what you have just read sounds like a fairytale because it is too easy, remember that if something sounds too good to be true, that is because it is not true.)

Sometimes it is easier to do something for yourself. Asking for donations might look easy but being successful at this means understanding the complexity of both motivation and ability, at the three levels of the individual, the social interaction of a community and an organization. Getting donations means requires mastering those six aspects of influence. For example, using personal motivation successfully to generate donation income means being able to make an appeal to 'values.' Achieving the second step means managing the complicated relationship between those six elements, the three levels of motivation and ability. Not easy ...

Instead of just chasing online donations, student members of STUDY FOR TWO used the web to recycle something they had plenty of: textbooks. Once STUDY FOR TWO collects used textbooks from university students before reselling them to other students at a low price, more than 80% of their earnings goes to children in developing countries. The web is also used for training courses, spreading ideas about how to collect and sell textbooks, and co-ordinate the plans of each branch: Tonkatsu (activities in Hokkaido, Tohoku and Chubu districts), Asakatsu

アイデアを行動に移すこ
とは？

個人で目標を達成するこ
とは？

ボランティア活動を評価
するには？

(morning activities of the Kanto district), Hirukatsu (lunchtime activities that take place in Kansai) and Kyukatsu (monthly activities in Kyushu). All of this information also creates interest in the annual Laos study tour program, which gives student volunteers the chance to visit the villages they support.

注：**non-profit organization** 非営利組織（団体）（NPO）　**generate donation income** 寄付による収益を生む　'**values**' 「道徳的価値観」

Comprehension Questions

Based on the Passage, please choose the best answer.

1. What does the first paragraph say about turning ideas into concrete actions?
    A. The happiest volunteers are students who teach in developing countries.
    B. Developing countries take concrete action for non-profit organizations.
    C. Children develop by researching internet education.
    D. Changing the world is more difficult than some fairytale where everything happens easily.

2. What does the second paragraph say about achieving your goals?
    A. Doing what you want to do as an individual is always the least difficult goal for an organization to achieve.
    B. Ability at the social interaction level means working as a team that achieves its own goals by donating to its own projects.
    C. Understanding the world of law is an important organizational ability.
    D. One difficult way to move forwards is to motivate people to give you money.

3. What does the third paragraph say about the best way to value volunteer activities?
    A. The best volunteer groups concentrate on chasing online donations.
    B. The best volunteer groups spend most of their earnings helping other people, connecting volunteers with the people being supported.
    C. The best volunteer groups work in the morning and rest in the afternoon.
    D. The best volunteer groups buy themselves lunch on a once-a-month tour, using the web to find interesting villages to support.

Dialogue

次の対話を聞いて，下線部を埋めてみよう．

Oscar: That really warmed me up. Could I have a ₁_____ please?

Nico: Sure, no problem. All part of ₂_____!

Oscar: I'm sorry to have to ₃_____ but I seem to be having some

₄_____ ...

Nico: OK. Would it help if you ₅_____ your computer in here?

Oscar: Actually, that would be a great help. Thank you.

Nico: You're welcome.

TOEIC Challenge

Based on the Dialogue, choose the best answer.

1. What problem does Oscar have?

   A. Oscar has no computer.

   B. Oscar's computer is broken.

   C. Oscar's computer battery is dead.

   D. Oscar cannot turn off the battery.

2. In which season do you think this dialogue occurred?

   A. In spring

   B. In summer

   C. In fall

   D. In winter

Useful Expressions for Conversation

1. お願いがあることを丁寧に伝える：用事を頼む前の根回し的表現

   次の文の中で，依頼の前置きとして最も丁寧な表現はどれですか？

   a. I have something to ask you.

   b. I have a favor to ask you.

   c. Can I ask you a favor?

   d. I was wondering if you could do me a favor.

2. 提案：「こうしたらいいんじゃないですか？」と提案する表現

   次の文の中で，相手に提案をする表現はどれですか？

   a. May I help you?

   b. Would it help if I drive you to the station?

   c. I'm happy to help.

d.   Please help yourself to the cake.

Practical Use

以下の下線部に日本文の意味に合うように適切な語（句）を入れ, その後, ペアで読んでみましょう.

1. 「会議室の予約をお願いしたいのですが.」
   "I'm _____ you could book a meeting room?"

   「もちろんいいですよ. 時間はどれくらいですか？」
   "No problem. What time do you need the room?"

2. 「悪いんだけど熱っぽいんだ.」
   "Sorry but I'm feeling _____."

   「じゃあ君の代わりに僕が彼女を迎えに行ってあげようか？」
   "Well, would it _____ I picked her up for you?"

Little Quiz

1. 英語の volunteer は, Longman Dictionary of Contemporary English によれば, "someone who does a job willingly without being paid" の意味です. すなわち, 「自ら進んで無報酬で仕事をする人」のことです. では, 以下のボランティアに関連する日本語を英語にしてみましょう.

   a.   ボランティアグループ
   b.   ボランティア活動
   c.   ボランティア活動をする
   d.   ボランティア休暇
   e.   ボランティア精神
   f.   ボランティア教育
   g.   バザーを手伝ってくれる有志の人
   h.   学校行事のお手伝いを進んで申し出る

2. 日本あるいは海外にはどのようなボランティア活動があるのかを調べて, あなたが興味をもったボランティア活動があれば, その活動内容を紹介してみましょう.

Unit 12

Changing the world: one friend at a time ...

Vocabulary Quiz

空所に入れるのに適した単語を，a～dの中から選び丸をつけましょう.

1. break the _____ （進行を妨げるものを解消する）
   a. bottlebrush   b. bottle cap   c. bottleneck   d. bottle nose
2. physical _____ （肉体的魅力）
   a. charm   b. charmed   c. charming   d. charmer
3. life _____ （余命）
   a. expectant   b. expectancy   c. expectation   d. expectative
4. _____ destiny （運命に抵抗する）
   a. resist   b. sustain   c. withstand   d. survive
5. an _____ life （冒険的な生活）
   a. adventure   b. adventurer   c. adventurism   d. adventurous
6. _____ a famous singer （有名な歌手を呼び物にする）
   a. feature   b. characterize   c. attract   d. call

Grammar Check

1. 次の分数を英語で読んでみましょう.

   $\frac{1}{2}$ _____

   $\frac{1}{3}$ { one/a } _____

   $\frac{2}{3}$ two- _____

   $3\frac{3}{4}$ three _____ three-_____

2. 「息を呑むほど美しい景色（シーン）」を表す英語として次の下線部には，それぞれ scene と scenery のいずれが入りますか？

   a breathtaking _____
   a breathtaking piece of _____

Changing the world, the people in it, or our place in the world are all big challenges that we will have to face as we move from the comfort of being a student to becoming a taxpayer. Changing ourselves can seem difficult when we are caught in the rhythm of being a student: how can we move in the world differently, how can we change what we do? Knowing that a chain is only as strong as its weakest link, and understanding what is limiting us is the start of changing ourselves. For most people, *who* you know shapes *what* you know and what you can *do*. Breaking the bottleneck of what is stopping us from moving ahead can sometimes start just by changing who we know.

自分自身を変えるには？

The student group NEIGHBOR is an international student group in Tokyo that brings the world closer by connecting students with people across the lines of generation, nationality and race. Japanese students learn more about the world as they explain the charms of life in Japan to foreigners. Japanese students know that the average Japanese life expectancy is 83 years old, and they learn that life in Zimbabwe is nearly half that at just 42 years. The Sahara Desert is more than 25 times larger than Japan, and the Bhutan population is one twelfth of the population of Tokyo. NEIGHBOR emphasizes that the world is full of difference as they ask students to resist the narrow perspective of Japanese common sense.

学生グループ NEIGHBOR とは？

Some events organized by NEIGHBOR feel more like an at-home party where connections are more important than Japanese. Forming teams that mix Japanese university students, foreign exchange students, students of Japanese language schools, and adult members of society means playing games like a world quiz does more than help Japanese students to become more interested in the world outside Japan. Other events are more simple because they are adventurous walking events shared with 120 foreigners from more than 40 countries or they feature sunsets and night views of famous locations, allowing participants to talk as they enjoy the scenery. Remarkable experiences like these NEIGHBOR events don't just happen. They are the result of being carefully planned by the organizers and participants intentionally recognizing the chance to make new and meaningful friendships.

学生グループ NEIGHBOR の活動は？

注：**breaking the bottleneck** ボトルネック（進行の妨げとなるもの・障害）を解消する

Comprehension Questions

Based on the Passage, please choose the best answer.

1. What does the first paragraph say about changing yourself?
   A. People who can't face the big challenges of making the world better should pay more taxes.
   B. The rhythm of study, part-time job and circle activities make it easy for students to change.
   C. The strongest link to personal change is the comfort we feel with our place in the world.
   D. Making new relationships with different people can change how we think and act.

2. What does the second paragraph say about the process of learning about the outside world?
   A. It is a great chance to explain why life in Japan is so interesting.
   B. Life is too short to worry about understanding foreign countries.
   C. Japanese desserts are the sweetest things in a world is full of difference.
   D. Japanese common sense is beautiful, not common.

3. What does the third paragraph say about the importance of social connections?
   A. The best meetings are those that just happen, without any planning.
   B. Friendship does not need teamwork because it happens naturally.
   C. Event planning is important if people are going to start important new relationships.
   D. The game of friendship develops like a mysterious adventure.

Dialogue

次の対話を聞いて，下線部を埋めてみよう.

Hanna: Before we get out on the water, ₁_____ you one difference. When you are out in your canoe, you have to ₂_____ as you paddle, right?

Lyle: Uh-huh.

Hanna: But because you are standing up, the idea is to ₃_____.

Lyle: I see. So, ₄_____ using the strength of my arms like I would in a canoe, I use the length of the paddle and my body weight to ₅_____ through the water, I guess ...

Hanna: Exactly!

Based on the Dialogue, choose the best answer.

1. Who are the two people talking?
    A. An instructor and a visitor
    B. Two people shopping together
    C. A parent and a child
    D. a clerk and a guest

2. What are the speakers discussing?
    A. How stand-up paddling（SUP）is different from paddling a canoe
    B. How to buy a canoe
    C. How to swim
    D. How to stand in the canoe

Useful Expressions for Conversation

1. 許可：誰かが何かをすることを許可する表現.

    次の文の中で，許可を表わしていない表現はどれですか？

    a. Let me know when you will arrive in Fukuoka.
    b. Don't let me down.
    c. Let him have a chance to speak.
    d. I'll let you know later.

2. 同意：同意を表す表現.

    次の文の中で，"Exactly." のような同意を表す表現としては用いられないのはどれですか？

    a. Absolutely.
    b. That's it.
    c. That's that.
    d. You can say that again.

Practical Use

以下の下線部に日本文の意味に合うように適切な語（句）を入れ,その後,ペアで読んでみましょう.

1. 「もう一枚写真を撮らせてください.」
   "Let _____ ."

   「構いませんよ」
   "Fine / All right / Not at all."

2. 「本当に退屈な映画ですね.」
   "This is a very _____ movie, isn't it?"

   「全くその通りです.」
   "You can _____ ."

Little Quiz

日本のおとぎ話の一つの「一寸法師」に登場する主人公の身長は何 cm か知っていますか？さて,物の長さを測るとき,昔の人々は体の一部の長さを単位としていました. 例えば,「フィート」（1 フィート＝約 31cm, 三分の一ヤード）という単位は,英米人の足のかかとからつま先までの長さで,日本の「尺」（1 尺＝約 30cm）に相当します. この「尺」は親指と人差し指を広げた時の両指先間の長さです. では,次の単位は体のどの部分の長さを単位にしたのでしょうか？絵を描いたり,自分の身体を使ったりして,説明してみましょう.

1. 1 インチ（inch）＝約 2.5cm （12 分の 1 フィート）
2. 1 寸＝約 3cm
3. 1 束＝約 18cm
4. 1 ヤード（yard）＝約 0.91m
5. 1 マイル（mile）＝約 1.6km
6. 1 キュービット（cubit）＝約 17 〜 21 インチ
7. 1 ファゾム（fathom）（主に水深を測る）＝ 6 フィート, 183cm ＝ 1 尋

Living the green dream: Global Brigades, recyclemania

Vocabulary Quiz

空所に入れるのに適した単語を，a〜d の中から選び丸をつけましょう.

1. a kitchen _____ （台所の大掃除）
   a. cleanup　　b. clear　　　　c. cleanly　　　　d. cleaner

2. the next _____ （次の世代）
   a. generate　　b. generation　　c. generational　　d. generative

3. a dangerous _____ （危険な任務）
   a. mention　　b. mission　　c. session　　　　d. cushion

4. a _____ environmental business plan （継続維持できる環境ビジネス上の案件）
   a. sustain　　b. sustained　　c. sustaining　　d. sustainable

5. a job-_____ activity （就職活動）
   a. hunt　　b. hunter　　c. hunting　　　　d. hunted

6. social _____ （社会的公平性）
   a. equity　　b. equivalence　　c. equation　　d. equal

Grammar Check

1. 次の二つのタイプ（コンマの有無）の関係詞節を含む文において，John に二人の娘の他にもう一人娘がいた場合，いずれの文が適格になりますか？

   a. John has two daughters who live in Fukuoka.
   b. John has two daughters, who live in Fukuoka.

2. 「ベッドの下には何がいると思う？うちの猫だよ.」の下線部を英訳すると，次のいずれが適格だと思いますか？

   a. Our cat is under the bed.
   b. Under the bed our cat is.
   c. Under the bed is our cat.

All around the world, student groups are concerned about the environment. Some student groups work directly to improve their local environment by showing how recycling improves life on campus, finding places where students can work with town people on making compost, and organizing clean-ups in local parks. Student groups are also looking at national and international issues by making connections with other environmental organizations. Other student groups are concerned about the next generation, so they volunteer to teach environmental education in high schools, showing how community gardening projects are both fun and important for improving how people live in cities.

学生の団体が環境のために力を尽くしていることは？

When a group of Tokyo students wanted to create a structure for making Eco Money, they chose the name em Factory. The mission of em Factory is to have some impact on business from the perspective of environmental issues. Finding answers to environmental problems requires raising students who have an environmental business perspective and can write sustainable environmental business plans for government and companies. Part of the success of em Factory as a job-hunting activity comes from their annual National Student Environmental Business Contest, which matches companies who have a concrete problem they want to solve with teams of students who have new ideas about how to think about such problems.

環境学生団体（em Factory）の環境ビジネス上の案件は？

As em Factory tries to resolve environmental problems from the perspective of business, students learn how business has evolved. In the late twentieth century, most companies were concerned with their 'bottom line', that very last line on a statement of revenue and expenses that records their financial profit or loss. From the 1960s onwards, the movement for corporate social responsibility (CSR, also called responsible business) meant that a growing number of companies were using a double bottom line system to measure the impact of the company. However, with the popularity of the sustainable business model (SBM), many companies now use a triple bottom line approach: the economic bottom line is concerned with

持続可能なビジネスモデル（SBM）に従い，多くの会社がとっているアプローチは？

profit; the social equity bottom line is concerned with people; and the environmental bottom line is concerned with the planet. At the heart of the em Factory mission is the need to turn 'waste' into profit.

注: **compost** 堆肥 **environmental organization** 環境保護団体 **community gardening projects** 地域のガーデニング事業 **National Student Environmental Business Contest**（環境学生団体 em Factory の）全国大学生環境ビジネスコンテスト **a statement of revenue and expenses** 収支計算書 **corporate social responsibility**（CSR）企業の社会的責任 **social equity** 社会の公平性

Comprehension Questions

Based on the Passage, please choose the best answer.

1. What does the first paragraph say about student groups working for the environment?
   A. Student groups are active at the local, national and international level.
   B. Student groups all over the world are selling the Big Issue magazine.
   C. Some student groups are using local education to make a greener future.
   D. Answers A and C are correct.

2. What does the second paragraph say about environmental business plans for government and companies?
   A. Student groups run the best factories for environmental business plans.
   B. Government and companies need environmental business plans that are sustainable.
   C. Raising students has a bigger environmental impact on companies than government rules.
   D. The government checks how each company concretely plans its job-hunting environment.

3. What does the third paragraph say about the changing realities of business?
   A. These days, thinking about anything other than profit is a waste.
   B. Responsible business means protecting company profits at all costs.
   C. Business today balances profits, people and the planet.
   D. The triple bottom line is about the planet, the planet and the planet.

Dialogue

次の対話を聞いて，下線部を埋めてみよう．

Otto: The bag was a red, patent leather, Gucci bag.

Ruby: You ₁_____ containing your passport and credit cards on the table when you went outside the restaurant to talk on your mobile phone, is that correct?

Otto: It ₂_____ I know, but yes, that is correct.

Ruby: If you ₃_____ your own belongings, you must not expect other people to cover your carelessness!

Otto: May I speak with my son now?

Ruby: There is one last question. ₄_____ you have lost a bag, I have written a report for your insurance company. ₅_____, I can accept that. But the third time means ....

TOEIC Challenge

Based on the Dialogue, choose the best answer.

1. Where did Otto leave the Gucci bag?
    A. At the entrance of the restaurant
    B. Outside the restaurant
    C. On a table in the restaurant
    D. On a table in the insurance company

2. How many times has Otto lost his bag, including this time?
    A. Once
    B. Twice
    C. Three times
    D. Four times

Useful Expressions for Conversation

1. 叱責：強い禁止を表す表現．

次の文の中で，強い禁止を表す表現はどれですか？

    a. You must not tell lies.
    b. You don't have to do your homework today.

   c. You may not smoke here.

   d. You cannot run here.

2. 許可を求める：許可を求める形式ばった表現.

   次の文の中で，上司，教員，年上の人等に対し，自分の中途退出の許可を求める表現はどれですか？

   a. Sorry to interrupt.

   b. Would you excuse me for a moment?

   c. Could you please leave the room?

   d. One minute, I'll be right back.

Practical Use

以下の下線部に日本文の意味に合うように適切な語（句）を入れ，その後，ペアで読んでみましょう.

1.「最近，電車の中で携帯電話で話す人を見かけます.」

   "I have recently seen ＿＿＿＿＿＿＿ their cell phone on the train."

   「車内では携帯電話の使用は控えてくださいとアナウンスがあるんだけどね.」

   "There is an announcement asking passengers ＿＿＿＿＿＿＿ talking on the cell phone on the train, though."

2.「君のノートパソコンを使って僕のメールをチェックしてもいいですか？」

   "＿＿＿＿＿＿ your laptop to check my email?"

   「どうぞご自由に.」

   "Be ＿＿＿＿＿."

Little Quiz

海外の企業や外資系企業への就職を希望する場合，英文履歴書（Resume または Curriculum Vitae（CV））が必要になってきます. では英文履歴書は和文履歴書とどのように異なっているのでしょうか？まず下記の中から，英文履歴書の記入に必要な項目と不要な項目とに分けてから，その相違を調べて発表してみましょう.

1. 個人データ：氏名，連絡先

2. 個人データ：生年月日，年齢，性別

3. 個人データ：顔写真

4. Objective（希望職種，職務）

5. 志望動機

6. Qualifications（資格，スキル）

7. Work Experience（職歴）

8. Education（学歴）

9. 個人データ：配偶者・子供の有無

10. 通勤時間

11. 履歴書の作成日

12. 印鑑

Rules: take, make, or break?

Vocabulary Quiz

空所に入れるのに適した単語を，a～dの中から選び丸をつけましょう．

1. a _____ of youth　　　　　　　　　　　（若さの特権）
   - a. privilege　　b. right　　　　c. special　　　　d. specialty
2. the _____ of marriages to divorces　（結婚と離婚の比率）
   - a. ratio　　　　b. ration　　　c. rational　　　d. rationale
3. the gender pay _____　　　　　　　　（男女の賃金格差）
   - a. gap　　　　　b. gape　　　　c. gapped　　　d. gag
4. be economically _____　　　　　　　（経済的に恵まれていない）
   - a. disadvantage　b. disadvantaged　c. disadvantageous　d. disadvantageously
5. a terrific _____　　　　　　　　　　（素晴らしい人材）
   - a. ability　　　b. competence　c. talent　　　d. faculty
6. _____ ahead　　　　　　　　　　　（進出する，成功する）
   - a. go　　　　　b. look　　　　c. remain　　　d. get

Grammar Check

1. Once という語が「いったん～すると，...」という意味になるのは，次の文のいずれですか？

   a. I *once* lived in Saga.

   b. *Once* I was stopped by a policeman on the street.

   c. *Once* you make a decision, don't give up until the last minute.

2. 「十中八九」を英語で表すと，次のいずれが適格ですか？

   a. in nine cases in ten

   b. in nine cases out of ten

When you come into your English class late, you might be thinking "Being a student is tough." To succeed, you have to manage study, exam preparation and part-time work while having a social life. Next time you feel that you are having trouble with your homework because of your schedule, try remembering that in some countries less than two out of ten people have the privilege of university study. Not having enough food or water, or finally getting your first pair of shoes when you are 15, these are serious problems. On the other hand, being so busy with club activities that you forget to do your homework is not such a big drama. In the wider scale of things, it is more like a luxury and less like a problem.

大学生はつらいよ.

Gender is a spectrum but take a look around your university classroom and see if the gender ratio is unbalanced. When Japan ranked 110th out of 149 countries in a recent World Economic Forum Gender Gap Report, there were clear problems in the education and economic participation of Japanese women. Japan is one of only three OECD countries where more men study at universities than women, and Japan has the third highest pay gap between men and women in OECD countries.

男女平等？

Noting that Japanese women are disadvantaged in both education and employment, a recent IMF report said that economic gender parity could add up to US$550 billion to Japanese GDP. Despite the fact that most of the highly skilled talent of university graduates around the world is actually held by women, nine out of ten Japanese men with university degrees work full time but only 71% of university-educated Japanese women work. When you see women in your university classroom, remember that once they graduate, they must choose between being a rule-taker who follows a system which stops women from getting ahead, or being a rule-breaker who takes on the challenge of getting past gender bias in the Japanese workplace. Once enough rule-breaking Japanese women move past the glass ceiling and become rule-makers, Japanese society will be stronger ... in about 30 years time.

日本人女性が直面する問題とは？

注： **in the wider scale of things** 全体像を考慮に入れると **a spectrum** スペクトル（境界線・範囲が明確でない状態が連続している様子のこと） **OECD** (**Organization for Economic Co-operation and Development**) 経済協力開発機構 **pay gap** 賃金格差 **IMF** (**International Monetary Fund**) 国際通貨基金 **GDP** (**Gross Domestic Product**) 国内総生産 **the glass ceiling** （企業等で女性や少数民族の昇進を阻む）目に見えない障壁

Based on the Passage, please choose the best answer.

1. What does the first paragraph say about problems?

   A. Most problems can be prevented by being on time.

   B. The best way to get ready for exams is to have a heavy part-time work schedule.

   C. Toilets, education, healthcare, and internet are basic needs.

   D. Not having the basic needs of food, water and clothing is a real problem.

2. What does the second paragraph say about the problems facing Japanese women?

   A. Confused and unbalanced: Facebook has 39 gender options for Japanese women.

   B. Japan is in the top fifty countries for how Japanese women study and work.

   C. Japan is outstanding: Japanese women are paid much less than Japanese men.

   D. University-educated Japanese women are the third-highest paid OECD group.

3. What does the third paragraph say about the impact of the problems facing Japanese women?

   A. If gender bias disappeared, the Japanese economy would improve dramatically.

   B. Japanese women are not paid enough for teaching OECD university graduates.

   C. The work of university-educated Japanese women would create more than US$550 billion each year.

   D. Many Japanese women are proud of the perfectly clean glass ceiling of Japan.

Dialogue

次の対話を聞いて，下線部を埋めてみよう．

Boaz:　I might need ₁＿＿＿＿＿＿＿ . I am a ₂＿＿＿＿＿, you see …

Opal:　OK, so, if cheese is fine, I can make you a pizza with plenty of vegetables. [checking while making an offer] What about salami?

Boaz:　Those sausages you slice up look ₃＿＿＿＿＿ for me, so perhaps I had better let someone else enjoy them. Could you ₄＿＿＿＿＿＿ , please?

Opal:　One medium pizza, full of vegetables, ₅＿＿＿＿＿＿ !

TOEIC Challenge

Based on the Dialogue, choose the best answer.

1. Where are these people talking?

   A. In a library

   B. On the telephone

   C. In a travel agency

   D. In a pizza parlor

2. What kind of pizza will Boaz probably eat?

   A. Pizza with variety of toppings

   B. Vegetarian pizza

   C. Pepperoni pizza

   D. Cheese pizza with sausage

Useful Expressions for Conversation

1. 同意：相手に同意を求める表現.

   次の文の you see の用法の中で，相手に同意を求めて，「〜だよね」の意味のカジュアルな表現はどれですか？

   a. *You see*, my tongue is sensitive to heat.

   b. Where do *you see* yourself in 10 years?

   c. The pennant race, *you see*, is heating up.

   d. The pennant race is coming to an end, *you see*.

2. 意見を求める：相手に対して意見を尋ねる表現として，適切なのはどれですか？

   a. What do you think about this plan?

   b. May I have your comment on this plan?

   c. What would you say if he changed this plan?

   d. What's your take on this plan?

以下の下線部に日本文の意味に合うように適切な語（句）を入れ，その後，ペアで読んでみましょう．

1. 「私，辛いものが苦手なのよね.」

   "I cannot handle spicy food, _____."

   「騙されたと思って，食べてご覧.　きっと気に入るよ.」
   "Take my word for it and _____ some!　I think you'll like it."

2. 「このレストラン，どう思う？」

   "_____ do you think about this restaurant?"

   「ええ，豪華ですね，彼女の誕生パーティーにピッタリですね.」
   "Well, I think it's very gorgeous.　It's _____ her birthday party."

Little Quiz

欧米社会では，男女平等の精神から性別を特定しない gender-neutral expression（性的に中立な表現）が好んで用いられます．例えば，三人称単数の代名詞の he / she の代わりに they が用いられるのもその理由からです．では，次の語を gender-neutral expression に代えてみましょう．

1. stewardess / steward
2. waitress / waiter
3. policewoman / policeman
4. actress / actor
5. spokeswoman / spokesman
6. fireman
7. postman, mailman
8. mankind
9. man-made
10. freshman
11. Mr., Ms., Mrs., Miss
12. hero / heroine

Unit 15

Hope is a senseless act of beauty: history is full of hope

Vocabulary Quiz

空所に入れるのに適した単語を，a〜dの中から選び丸をつけましょう.

1. a machine _____ by electricity　　　　　　（電動式の機械）
   a. controlled　　b. assembled　　c. installed　　d. driven

2. _____ a difference　　　　　　（相違を生じる）
   a. make　　　　b. take　　　　c. have　　　　d. do

3. _____ of stimuli　　　　　　（刺激の貧困）
   a. poor　　　　b. lack　　　　c. poverty　　　d. difficulty

4. _____ ideas　　　　　　（具体的な考え）
   a. abstract　　b. concrete　　c. conscious　　d. complete

5. build _____ his plan　　　　　　（彼のプランを推し進める）
   a. in　　　　　b. on　　　　c. into　　　　d. up

6. a _____ effect　　　　　　（波及効果）
   a. ripple　　　b. wave　　　c. babble　　　d. bubble

Grammar Check

1. 「互いに罵り合う」を英語にすると，次のいずれが適格ですか？

   a. shout and scream each other
   b. shout and scream at each other

2. while が動作や状態が並行していることを表し，「〜している間に」の意味は次のいずれですか？

   a. Taro likes English while Bob likes Japanese.
   b. The phone rang while I was taking a shower.

Being a student means you want to change things. You want to change yourself, and you hope to change your position in the world. And by doing that, you also want to change the world. Each time you come to class or take an exam, you are using hope to get you from where you are to somewhere new. Regarding COVID, history tells us that this is not our first epidemic. Hope is important, not only for people like us, but for all of Japanese society, as we move together towards a brighter future after COVID.

希望とは？

Hope can drive the way we think, feel, and act as we try to co-exist with the coronavirus. But changing ourselves while that virus is also limiting what is possible in our world seems to be so difficult that we sometimes even forget to take the first step. Using hope to take one small step at a time does make a difference to the future. Muhammed Yunus, the Nobel Prize winner who lifted thousands of people from poverty by giving them business loans without collateral, began with less than three thousand yen. When Muhammed combined his hope for a better world with that money, it was enough to help 42 people start their own business.

希望を持てば出来ること
は？

When you look around where you live, work and play, what local issue needs more attention? Once you have taken that first step of changing hope for a better future into doing something concrete, your small actions can build on each other. While sharing information with your friends to highlight the issue, try practicing random acts of COVID kindness. Simple things like always carrying a spare mask to give to anyone who needs it, helping an older person in your neighborhood with their wi-fi setup so they won't feel so isolated during lockdowns, or finding some neighborhood activity you and your friends like to do for charity, these actions start a ripple effect that can carry from one person to another, making someone's lockdown day a little bit brighter. As we learn more about how to live in the age of COVID, the level of hope that people feel each day can be strengthened by caring social networks. Carry it forwards: investing in the hope of those around us is one way to gently help them to help us change the world.

希望を持つ効果は？

注：**business loans without collateral** 無担保貸付金　**practicing random acts of COVID kindness** コロナウィルス感染症で困ったときはお互いさま（人々の親切心を広める行動）　**caring** 思いやりのある　**carry it forwards** 先に進める（pay it forward「先に払う」と同じ意味，つまり各人が互いに無償奉仕をしあう，親切の輪を広げていく，という意味）

Comprehension Questions

Based on the Passage, please choose the best answer.

1. What does the first paragraph say about hope?

    A. Hope is private.

    B. Hope is public.

    C. Hope is public and private.

    D. Haters don't hope.

2. What does the second paragraph say about what hope can do?

    A. Hope is all we need to make change happen.

    B. If hope is the steering wheel of a car, then action is the brake.

    C. Hope is the business of winning one prize after another.

    D. Connecting hope and a series of small actions can change the world.

3. What does the third paragraph say about the impact of hope?

    A. The impact of hope is increased by helping others to feel hopeful about their future.

    B. Our private hope becomes public when we share it by caring for other people.

    C. Both of the above are correct.

    D. Pay it forward means borrow now and hope to pay it back after poverty is behind you.

Dialogue （31）

次の対話を聞いて，下線部を埋めてみよう.

Ida: So, how far ₁_____ are you?

Hopper: Well ... at least a week ...

Ida: You mean, the thesis is ₂_____ and right now, you don't even know how bad your problem is?

Hopper: Uh-huh.

Ida: Oh no. Well, let's ₃_____ of what you must do and ₄_____ it, OK?

Hopper: Sure.

Ida: You know, I have recently enjoyed paying for your tuition, knowing that you can do this. [expressing pride] You just need to get ₅_____ and it will be fine ...

TOEIC Challenge

Based on the Dialogue, choose the best answer.

1. Who is Ida?

   A. A parent of Hopper

   B. A friend of Hopper

   C. A professor of Hopper

   D. A counselor of Hopper

2. When is the deadline for Hopper's thesis?

   A. One week later

   B. Two weeks later

   C. Three weeks later

   D. One month later

Useful Expressions for Conversation

1. 確認：相手の真意を確認する表現.

    次の文の中で，相手の真意を確認する表現はどれですか？

    a. You mean ～ ?
    b. Get it?
    c. I mean ～ .
    d. You don't say!

2. 確認：相手の理解を期待して，内容を確認する表現.
    相手はその内容に関して知っているという前提がある際に用いられる.「ご存知の通り，～なんですよ.」という意味のカジュアルな表現.

    次の you know の用法の中で，相手の理解を期待して，「あなたもご存じの通り，～なんですよ」という意味の，内容を確認する表現はどれですか？

    a. *You know* what I mean?
    b. *You know*, money cannot buy happiness.
    c. We went to the Chinese restaurant at Tenjin, *you know*, "Shanghai Hanten."
    d. We have to study the way to use honorifics, *you know*.

以下の下線部に日本文の意味に合うように適切な語（句）を入れ, その後, ペアで読んでみましょう.

1. 「プールに泳ぎに行くのはいやです.」

"I hate to go swimming in the pool."

「金づちだからということですね.」

"_____ you swim like _____."

2. 「いいかい, キャンセル待ちで行くしかないよね.」

"_____ , we have no choice to go on standby."

「仕方ないことですね.」

"It cannot be _____."

Little Quiz

日本語で「私の手がとても冷たい」場合に「私の手は氷のように冷たい」のように直喩（simile）と呼ばれる比喩の一種が用いられる場合があります. 英語では（as）～ as X や～ like X を用いて X に喩えるものをもってきます. この例の場合, 英語でも My hands are as cold as ice となり, 喩えるものは日英語で同じになります. では, 以下の直喩において, 喩える動物やモノは日英語で同じでしょうか, それとも異なるでしょうか, グループで話し合って, 発表してみましょう.

1. とても多忙である

   彼は～のように忙しい.　　　　He is as busy as _____.
2. ぐっすり眠り込む

   彼は～のように眠り込んだ.　　He slept like _____.
3. 性格が温和

   彼は～のようにやさしい.　　　He is as gentle as _____.
4. とても勇敢である

   あの人は～のように勇敢だ.　　That man is as brave as _____.
5. うぬぼれが強い.

   あの人は～のように得意げだ.　That man is as proud as _____.
6. 非常に憶病である

   彼は～のように臆病だ.　　　　He is as timid as _____.
7. とても賢い

   彼は～のように賢い.　　　　　He is as wise as _____.

8. 非常に静まり返っている

　　　この通りは〜のように静まり返っている．　This street is as silent as _____.

9. とても軽い．

　　　このバッグは〜のように軽い．　　　　　This bag is as light as _____.

10. 非常に堅固である

　　　この家は〜のように堅固だ．　　　　　　This house is as solid as _____.

テキストの音声は、弊社 HP　https://www.eihosha.co.jp/
の「テキスト音声ダウンロード」のバナーからダウンロードできます。
また、下記 QR コードを読み込み、音声ファイルをダウンロードするか、
ストリーミングページにジャンプして音声を聴くことができます。

Hope: Beyond Kyushu
日本から世界へ 発信するコミュニケーション

2024 年 1 月 15 日　初　版

編　著　者 ©久　保　善　宏
©Ｔｉｍ　Ｃｒｏｓｓ

発　行　者　佐　々　木　　　元

発　行　所　株式会社　英　宝　社

〒 101-0032 東京都千代田区岩本町 2-7-7
電話 03-5833-5870　FAX03-5833-5872
https://www.eihosha.co.jp/

ISBN 978-4-269-17032-2 C1082
印刷・製本：日本ハイコム株式会社